What Readers Are Saying About *Programming Scala*

This books speaks directly to developers faced with the real and hard problems of concurrency. It offers clear solutions for building actors on the JVM.

► **John Heintz**
Principal, Gist Labs

Venkat introduces (Java) developers to programming Scala in an easy-to-follow, pragmatic style. This book covers Scala from basics to concurrency, one of the most critical and most difficult topics in programming today. Venkat gets to the meat without any fluff, and I highly recommend this book to get you up to speed on Scala quickly.

► **Scott Leberknight**
Chief architect, Near Infinity Corporation

Once again Venkat has made learning easy and fun. With his conversational style, this book allows developers to quickly learn the Scala language, its uniqueness, and how it can be best utilized in a multi-language environment.

► **Ian Roughley**
Consultant, Down & Around, Inc.

Multicore processors demand that developers have a solid grounding in the functional programming concepts found at the core of Scala. Venkat provides a great guide to get you started with this exciting new language.

► **Nathaniel T. Schutta**
Author, speaker, teacher

A pleasure to read! A great introduction to Scala for the experienced Java developer! This book teaches the "Scala way" of programming from a Java, object-oriented perspective. Very thorough yet concise.

► **Albert Scherer**
Software architect, Follett Higher Education Group, Inc.

Concurrency is the next giant challenge we must face as developers, and traditional imperative languages make it too hard. Scala is a functional language on the JVM that offers easy multithreading, concise syntax, and seamless Java interop. This book guides Java developers through the important capabilities and nuances of Scala, showing why so much interest is bubbling around this new language.

▶ **Neal Ford**
Software architect/meme wrangler, ThoughtWorks, Inc.

Programming Scala is concise, easy to read, and thorough...one of the best introductions to Scala currently available. It's a must-read for the programmer who wants to stay relevant as we enter the era of ubiquitous multicore processing. This is one of the books that I will go back to, time and again, in the coming years.

▶ **Arild Shirazi**
Senior software developer, CodeSherpas, Inc.

Programming Scala

Tackle Multicore Complexity on the JVM

Programming Scala
Tackle Multicore Complexity on the JVM

Venkat Subramaniam

The Pragmatic Bookshelf
Raleigh, North Carolina   Dallas, Texas

Many of the designations used by manufacturers and sellers to distinguish their products are claimed as trademarks. Where those designations appear in this book, and The Pragmatic Programmers, LLC was aware of a trademark claim, the designations have been printed in initial capital letters or in all capitals. The Pragmatic Starter Kit, The Pragmatic Programmer, Pragmatic Programming, Pragmatic Bookshelf and the linking *g* device are trademarks of The Pragmatic Programmers, LLC.

Every precaution was taken in the preparation of this book. However, the publisher assumes no responsibility for errors or omissions, or for damages that may result from the use of information (including program listings) contained herein.

Our Pragmatic courses, workshops, and other products can help you and your team create better software and have more fun. For more information, as well as the latest Pragmatic titles, please visit us at

    http://www.pragprog.com

Printed in the United States of America.

ISBN-10: 1-934356-31-X

ISBN-13: 978-1-934356-31-9

Printed on acid-free paper.

P1.0 printing, June 2009

Version: 2009-6-16

Contents

Chapter 1

Introduction

There are so many languages that you could use to program the JVM. In this book I hope to convince you to take the time to learn Scala.

The Scala language has been designed for concurrency, expressiveness, and scalability. The language and its libraries let you focus on your problem domain without being bogged down by low-level infrastructure details like threads and synchronization.

We live in a world where hardware is getting cheaper and more powerful. Users now have devices with multiple processors, each with multiple cores. Although Java has served us well so far, it was not designed to take advantage of the power we have on hand today. Scala lets you put all that power to use to create highly responsive, scalable, performing applications.

In this introduction, we'll take a quick tour of the benefits of functional programming and Scala to show you what makes Scala attractive. In the rest of this book, you'll learn how to use Scala to realize those benefits.

1.1 Why Scala?

Is Scala the right language for you?

Scala is a hybrid functional and object-oriented language. When creating a multithreaded application in Scala, you'll lean toward a functional style of programming where you write lock-free code with *immutable* state.[1] Scala provides an actor-based message-passing model that removes the pain associated with concurrency. Using this model, you can write concise multithreaded code without the worries of data contention between threads and the resulting nightmare of dealing with locks and releases. You can retire the synchronized keyword from your vocabularies and enjoy the productivity gains of Scala.

The benefits of Scala, however, are not limited to multithreaded applications. You can also use it to build powerful, concise, single-threaded applications and single-threaded modules of multithreaded applications. You can quickly put to use the powerful capabilities of Scala, including sensible static typing, closures, immutable collections, and elegant pattern matching.

Scala's support for functional programming helps you to write concise and expressive code. Thanks to the higher level of abstraction, you can get more things done with fewer lines of code. The functional style will benefit both your single-threaded applications and your multithreaded applications.

A number of functional programming languages exist. Erlang, for one, is a nice functional programming language. In fact, Scala's concurrency model is very similar to that of Erlang. However, Scala has two significant advantages over Erlang. First, Scala is strongly typed, while Erlang is not. Second, unlike Erlang, Scala runs on the JVM and interoperates very well with Java.

These two features of Scala make it a prime candidate for use in different layers of enterprise applications. You can certainly use Scala to build an entire enterprise application if you desire. Alternately, you can use it in different layers along with other languages. You can take advantage of the strong typing, superb concurrency model, and powerful pattern matching capabilities in layers where they would matter the most in your applications. The following figure, inspired by Ola Bini's Language Pyramid (see "Fractal Programming" in Appendix A, on page 207), shows where Scala may fit in with other languages in an enterprise application.

---

1. An object is said to be *immutable* if you can't change its contents once you create it. This eliminates the concerns of managing contention when multiple threads access the object. Java's String is a great example of an immutable object.

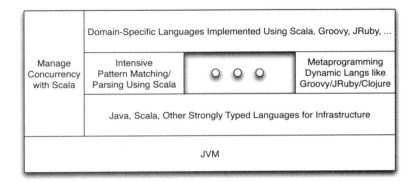

What about other languages on the JVM...Groovy, JRuby, Clojure?

Scala is by far the only prominent strongly typed language that provides functional style and great concurrency support. JRuby and Groovy are dynamic languages. They are not functional and do not provide any more solutions for concurrency than Java does. Clojure, on the other hand, is a hybrid functional language. It is dynamic in nature and so is not statically typed. Furthermore, its syntax is similar to Lisp, which is not the easiest syntax to work with unless you are familiar with it.

If you are an experienced Java programmer and are battling with Java to implement multithreaded applications, you will find Scala to be very useful. You can quite easily wrap your Java code into Scala's actors to provide thread isolation. To communicate between the threads, you can use Scala's lightweight API to easily pass messages. Instead of launching threads and immediately limiting concurrency by synchronization, you can use lock-free message passing to enjoy true concurrency.

If you value static typing and like to benefit from the support offered by the compiler, you will find that the static typing provided in Scala works for you without standing in your way. You will enjoy typing without having to type as much code.

If you are looking for a higher level of abstraction and highly expressive code, you'll be attracted to Scala's conciseness. You can get a lot more done with less code in Scala. You will also find the flexibility of Scala when it comes to operators and notations useful for creating domain-specific languages.

There is a caveat, however. Scala's conciseness at times leans toward terseness, which can make it hard to understand the code. The operators and constructs of Scala can be quite intimidating[2] to a beginner. The syntax is not going to be easy for the faint of heart certainly. As you get proficient with Scala, though, you will begin to appreciate the conciseness and learn to avoid the terseness so the code is easier to maintain and understandable at the same time.

Scala is not an all-or-nothing proposition. You don't have to throw away the time, money, and effort you've invested writing Java code. You can intermix Scala with Java libraries. You can build full applications entirely in Scala or intermix it to the extent you desire with Java and other languages on the JVM. So, your Scala code could be as small as a script or as large as a full-fledged enterprise application. Scala has been used to build applications in various domains including telecommunications, social networking, semantic web, and digital asset management. Apache Camel uses Scala for its DSL to create routing rules. Lift WebFramework is a powerful web development framework built using Scala. It takes full advantage of Scala features such as conciseness, expressiveness, pattern matching, and concurrency.

1.2 What's Scala?

Scala, short for Scalable Language, is a hybrid functional programming language. It was created by Martin Odersky[3] and was first released in 2003. Here are some of the key features of Scala:[4]

- It has an event-based concurrency model.
- It supports both an imperative style and a functional style.
- It is purely object-oriented.
- It intermixes well with Java.
- It enforces sensible static typing.
- It is concise and expressive.
- It is built on a small kernel.
- It is highly scalable, and it takes less code to create high-performing applications.

---

2. I've never learned a language whose syntax did not hurt my head when I started out with it—Ruby included. Practice, and the syntax becomes natural fairly soon.
3. For more information, see "A Brief History of Scala" in Appendix A, on page 207.
4. Refer to "Scala Language Specification" in Appendix A, on page 207, for the definitive language specification.

Here is a quick example that highlights many of these features:

Introduction/TopStock.scala

```scala
import scala.actors._
import Actor._

val symbols = List( "AAPL", "GOOG", "IBM", "JAVA", "MSFT")
val receiver = self
val year = 2008

symbols.foreach { symbol =>
  actor { receiver ! getYearEndClosing(symbol, year) }
}

val (topStock, highestPrice) = getTopStock(symbols.length)

printf("Top stock of %d is %s closing at price %f\n", year, topStock, highestPrice)
```

Don't be distracted by the syntax. Focus on the big picture for now. symbols refers to an immutable list that holds stock ticker symbols. We loop through each of the symbols and invoke an *actor*. Scala actors execute in separate threads. So, the code block ({}) associated with the actor runs on its own thread. It invokes the (not yet implemented) function getYearEndClosing(). The result of this call is then sent back to the actor that initiated this request. This is done using the special bang symbol (!). Back in the main thread, we call the (not yet implemented) function getTopStock(). So, once the previous code is fully implemented, we can use it to look up stock closing prices concurrently.

Let's now take a look at the function getYearEndClosing():

Introduction/TopStock.scala

```scala
def getYearEndClosing(symbol : String, year : Int) = {
  val url = "http://ichart.finance.yahoo.com/table.csv?s=" +
    symbol + "&a=11&b=01&c=" + year + "&d=11&e=31&f=" + year + "&g=m"

  val data = io.Source.fromURL(url).mkString
  val price = data.split("\n")(1).split(",")(4).toDouble
  (symbol, price)
}
```

In this short and sweet function, we send a request to http://ichart.finance.yahoo.com and receive the stock data in CSV format. We then parse the data and extract the year-end closing price. Don't worry about the format of the data received right now. That is not important for what we're focusing on here. In Chapter 14, *Using Scala*, on page 183, I will revisit this example and provide all the details about talking to the Yahoo service.

We are left with implementing the getTopStock() method, which is the method in which we will receive the closing prices and determine the highest-priced stock. Let's see how we can do that in a functional style:

```scala
Introduction/TopStock.scala

def getTopStock(count : Int) : (String, Double) = {
  (1 to count).foldLeft("", 0.0) { (previousHigh, index) =>
    receiveWithin(10000) {
      case (symbol : String, price : Double) =>
        if (price > previousHigh._2) (symbol, price) else previousHigh
    }
  }
}
```

We wrote the getTopStock() method without a single explicit assignment operation to any variable. We took the number of symbols as a parameter to this method. Our goal is to find the symbol with the highest closing price. So, we start with the initial symbol and a high price of ("", 0.0) as a parameter to the foldLeft() method. We use the foldLeft() method to help compare the prices for each symbol and determine the highest. Using the receiveWithin() method, we receive the symbol and price values from the actors we started with. The receiveWithin() method will time out after the said interval if it did not receive any messages. As soon as we receive a message, we determine whether the price received is higher than the high price we currently have. If it is, we use the new symbol and its price as the high for comparison with the next price we will receive. Otherwise, we use the previously determined (previousHigh) symbol and high price. Whatever we return from the code block attached to foldLeft() is used as a parameter to the call into the block in the context of the next element. Finally, the symbol and the high price are returned from foldLeft(). Again, focus on the big picture, and do not worry about the details of each of the methods mentioned. I will discuss these in detail as we move through the book.

That was about twenty-five lines of code to concurrently access the Web in order to analyze the closing price of select ticker symbols. Spend a few minutes tracing through the code to make sure you understand how this is working. While at it, see how the method computed the highest price without ever changing any variable or object. The entire code is totally dealing with only immutable state; no variable or object was changed after it was created. As a result, you should not be concerned with any synchronization and data contention. There is also no need for explicit notify and wait sequences. The message send and receive took care of that implicitly.

If you put all the previous code together and execute, you will get the following output:

```
Top stock of 2008 is GOOG closing at price 307.650000
```

Assume the network delay is d seconds and you are interested in analyzing n symbols. If you wrote the code to run sequentially, that would take about n * d seconds. Since we executed the requests for data concurrently, the previous code takes only about d seconds. The biggest delay in the code will be network access, and we executed that concurrently, but without writing a lot of code and putting in a lot of effort.

Imagine how you would have implemented the previous example in Java.

The previous code is distinctive from how you'd implement it in Java in three significant ways:

- First, the code is concise. We took advantage of a number of powerful Scala features: actors, closures, collections, pattern matching, and tuples, to mention a few. Of course, I have not introduced any of these yet; you're only in the introduction! So, don't try to understand all of that at this moment, because you have the rest of the book for that.

- We communicated between threads using message passing. So, there was no need for wait() and notify(). If you were using the traditional thread API in Java, the code would be quite complex by a few orders of magnitude. The newer Java concurrency API relieves us of that burden by using the executor services. However, in comparison, you will find Scala's actor-based message model to be a lot simpler and easier to use.

- Since we handled only immutable state, we did not have to spend any time or effort (and sleepless nights) with data contention and synchronization.

These benefits have removed a huge burden from your shoulders. For an exhaustive treatise about how painful threads can be, refer to Brian Goetz's *Java Concurrency in Practice* [Goe06]. With Scala, you can focus on your application logic instead of worrying about the low-level threading concerns.

You saw the concurrency benefit of Scala. Scala concurrently (pun intended) provides benefits for single-threaded applications as well. Scala provides you with the freedom to choose and mix two styles of programming: the imperative style promoted in Java and the assign-mentless pure functional style. By allowing you to mix these two styles, Scala lets you use the style you're most comfortable with within the scope of a single thread. This also enables you to call into and intermix with existing Java code.

In Scala, everything is an object. For example, 2.toString() will generate a compilation error in Java. However, that is valid in Scala—we're calling the toString() method on an instance of Int. At the same time, in order to provide good performance and interoperability with Java, Scala maps the instances of Int to the 32-bit primitive int representation at the byte-code level.

Scala compiles down to bytecode. You can run it the same way you run programs written using the Java language.[5] You can also intermix it well with Java. You can extend Java classes from Scala classes, and vice versa. You can also use Java classes in Scala and Scala classes in Java. You can program applications using multiple languages and be a true Polyglot Programmer[6]—you can take advantage of Scala in Java applications where you need concurrency or conciseness (like creating domain-specific languages).

Scala is a statically typed language, but, unlike Java, it has sensible static typing. Scala applies type inference in places it can. So, instead of specifying the type repeatedly and redundantly, you can rely on the language to learn the type and enforce it through the rest of the code. You don't work for the compiler; instead, you let the compiler work for you. For example, when we define var i = 1, Scala immediately figures that the variable i is of type Int. Now, if we try to assign a String to that variable as in i = "haha", we will get a compilation error with the following message:

```
error: type mismatch;
 found   : java.lang.String("haha")
 required: Int
       i = "haha"
```

Later in this book you will see how type inference works beyond such simple definitions and transcends further to function parameters and return values.

---

5. You can also run it as a script.
6. See "Polyglot Programming" in Appendix A, on page 207, as well as Neal Ford's *The Productive Programmer* [For08].

Scala favors conciseness. Placing a semicolon at the end of statements is second-nature to Java programmers. Scala provides a break for your right pinky finger from the years of abuse it has taken—semicolons are optional in Scala. But, that is only the beginning. In Scala, depending on the context, the dot operator (.) is optional as well, and so are the parentheses. So, instead of writing s1.equals(s2);, we can write s1 equals s2. By losing the semicolon, the parentheses, and the dot, your code gains a high signal-to-noise ratio. It becomes easier to write domain-specific languages.

One of the most interesting aspects of Scala is *scalability*. You can enjoy a nice interplay of functional programming constructs along with the powerful Java libraries, and you can create highly scalable, concurrent Java applications to take full advantage of multithreading on multicore processors using the facilities provided in Scala.

The real beauty of Scala is in what it does not have. Compared to Java, C#, and C++, the Scala language has a very small kernel of rules built into it. The rest, including operators, are part of the Scala library. This distinction has a far-reaching consequence. Because the language does not do more, you are able to do a lot more with it. It is truly extensible, and its library serves as a case study for that.

1.3 Functional Programming

I've mentioned that Scala can be used as a functional programming language a couple of times already. I want to take a few pages to give you a little of the flavor of functional programming. Let's start by contrasting it with the imperative style of Java programming. If we want to find the maximum temperature for a given day, we could write Java code like this:

```
//Java code
public static int findMax(List<Integer> temperatures) {
  int highTemperature = Integer.MIN_VALUE;
  for(int temperature : temperatures) {
   highTemperature = Math.max(highTemperature, temperature);
  }
  return highTemperature;
}
```

We created the mutable variable highTemperature and continually modified it in the loop. When you have mutable variables, you have to ensure you initialize them properly and are changing them in the right place to the right values.

Functional programming is a declarative style in which you say what to do instead of how something should be done. You've used functional style if you've used XSLT, a rules engine, or ANTLR. We can rewrite the previous code in functional style with no mutable variables as follows:

`Introduction/FindMaxFunctional.scala`

```
def findMax(temperatures : List[Int]) = {
  temperatures.foldLeft(Integer.MIN_VALUE) { Math.max }
 }
```

You are seeing an interplay of Scala conciseness and functional programming style in the previous code. That's some dense code. Take a few minutes to let that sink in.

We created the function findMax() that accepts, as a parameter, an immutable collection of temperature values (temperatures). The = symbol between the parentheses and the curly brace told Scala to infer the return type of this function (in this case an Int).

Within the function, we asked the foldLeft() method of the collection to exercise the function Math.max() for each element of the collection. As you know, the max() method of the java.lang.Math class takes two parameters, which are the values we want to determine the maximum of. Those two parameters are being sent implicitly in the previous code. The first implicit parameter to max() is the previous high value, and the second parameter is the current element in the collection that foldLeft() is navigating or iterating over. foldLeft() takes the result of the call to max, which is the current high value, and sends it to the subsequent call to max() to compare with the next element. The parameter to foldLeft() is the initial value for the high temperature.

The foldLeft() method takes effort to grasp. Assume for a minute that the elements in the collection are people who form a line and that we want to find the age of the oldest person. We write 0 on a note and give it to the first person in the line. The first person discards the note (because he's older than age 0); creates a new note with his age, 20; and hands the slip to the next person in line. The second person, who is younger than 20, simply passes the note to the person next to him. The third person, who is 32, discards the note and creates a new one to pass along. The note we get from the last person will contain the age of the oldest person in the line. Visualize this sequence, and you know what foldLeft() does under the covers.

Did the previous code feel like taking a shot of Red Bull? Scala code is highly concise and can be intense. You have to put in some effort to learn the language. But once you do, you will be able to take advantage of its power and expressiveness.

Let's take a look at another example of functional style. Suppose we want a list whose elements are double the values in an original list. Rather than loop through each element to realize that, we simply say we want elements doubled and let the language do the looping, as shown here:

```
Introduction/DoubleValues.scala
```

```scala
val values = List(1, 2, 3, 4, 5)

val doubleValues = values.map(_ * 2)
```

Read the keyword val as *immutable*. We are telling Scala that the variables values and doubleValues can't be changed once created.

Although it may not look like it, _ * 2 is a function. It is an anonymous function, which means it's a function with only a body but no name. The underscore (_) represents the argument passed to this function. The function itself is passed as an argument to the map function. The map() function iterates over the collection and, for each element in the collection, invokes the anonymous function given as a parameter. The overall result is a new list consisting of elements that are double those in the original list.

See how can you treat functions (in this case the one that doubles a number) just like regular parameters and variables? Functions are first-class citizens in Scala.

So, although we obtained a list with double the values of elements in the original list, we did so without modifying any variable or object. This immutable approach is a key concept that makes functional programming a desirable style for concurrent programming. In functional programming, functions are pure. The output they produce is based solely on the input they receive, and they are not affected by or affect any state, global or local.

1.4 What's in This Book?

My objective in writing this book is to get you up to speed on Scala so you can use it to write concurrent, scalable, expressive programs. There is a lot you need to learn to do that, but there is a lot more you don't need to know as well. If your objective is to learn everything that there is to learn about Scala, you will not find that in this book. There is already a book called *Programming in Scala* [OSV08] by Martin Odersky, Lex Spoon, and Bill Venners that does a great job of introducing the language in great depth. What you will see in this book are essential concepts that you need to know to start using Scala.

I assume you are quite familiar with Java. So, you will not learn basic concepts of programming from this book. However, I do not assume you have knowledge of functional programming or the Scala language itself—you will learn that in this book.

I have written this book for a busy Java developer, so my objective is to make you comfortable with Scala quickly so you can start building parts of your application with it really soon. You will see that the concepts are introduced fairly quickly but with lots of examples.

The rest of the book is organized as follows.

In each chapter, you'll learn essential facts that will get you closer to writing concurrent code in Scala.

I will walk you through installing Scala and getting your first Scala code executed in Chapter 2, *Getting Started*, on page 17. I'll show you how to run Scala as a script, how to compile it like traditional Java code, and how to run it using the java tool.

In Chapter 3, *Getting Up to Speed in Scala*, on page 25, you'll get a quick tour of Scala, its conciseness, how it deals with Java classes and primitives, and how it adds flavor to what you already have in Java. Scala also has some surprises for the unsuspecting Java programmer, as you'll see in this chapter.

Scala, being a pure object-oriented language, handles classes quite differently than Java. For instance, it has no static keyword, yet you can create class members using companion objects. You'll learn Scala's way of OO programming in Chapter 4, *Classes in Scala*, on page 45.

Scala is a statically typed language. It provides compile-time checking without the heavyweight ceremonial[7] syntax of other statically typed languages. In Chapter 5, *Sensible Typing*, on page 55, you'll learn about Scala's lightweight sensible typing.

Function values and closures are central concepts in functional programming and one of the most common features in Scala. In Chapter 6, *Function Values and Closures*, on page 67, I will walk you through examples of how you can put this to good use.

In Chapter 7, *Traits and Type Conversions*, on page 83, you will learn how to abstract behavior that can be mixed into arbitrary classes and about Scala's implicit type conversion.

Scala provides both mutable and immutable collections. You can create them concisely and iterate through them using closures, as you'll see in Chapter 8, *Using Collections*, on page 95.

In Chapter 9, *Pattern Matching and Regular Expressions*, on page 109, you will explore facilities for pattern matching, one of the most powerful features of Scala and the one you'll rely on in concurrent programming.

When you get to Chapter 10, *Concurrent Programming*, on page 125, you have arrived at the feature you've been waiting for in this book. You will learn about the powerful event-based concurrency model and the actor API to support it.

Once you figure out how to use concurrency, you'll want to put it to use in your Java applications. Chapter 11, *Intermixing with Java*, on page 151 will show you how to do that.

You want to make sure the code you type does what you want. Scala has good support for unit testing. You'll learn how to use JUnit, TestNG, or a Scala-based testing tool for testing Scala and Java code in Chapter 12, *Unit Testing with Scala*, on page 163.

I know you write superb code. However, you will still have to deal with exceptions that arise from the code you call. Scala takes a different approach to exception handling than Java does, as you'll see in Chapter 13, *Exception Handling*, on page 179.

In Chapter 14, *Using Scala*, on page 183, I will bring together the concepts in this book and show how you can put Scala to good use for building real-world applications.

---

7. See "Essence vs. Ceremony" in Appendix A, on page 207.

Finally, in Appendix A, on page 207, you'll find references to articles and blogs on the Web referenced in this book.

1.5 Who Is This Book For?

This book is for experienced Java programmers. I assume you are quite familiar with the Java language syntax and the Java API. I also assume you have strong object-oriented programming knowledge. These assumptions will allow you to quickly get into the essence of Scala and make use of it on real applications.

Developers who are familiar with other languages can use this book as well but will have to supplement it with good Java books.

Programmers who are somewhat familiar with Scala can use this book to learn some language features that they may not otherwise have had the opportunity to explore. Those already familiar with Scala can use this book for training fellow programmers in their organizations.

1.6 Acknowledgments

I had the privilege of getting help from some really smart minds when writing this book. These highly passionate people with very busy schedules volunteered their time to critique this book, tell me where I fell short, tell me where I did well, and encourage me along the way. This is a better book thanks to Al Scherer, Andres Almiray, Arild Shirazi, Bill Venners, Brian Goetz, Brian Sam-bodden, Brian Sletten, Daniel Hinojosa, Ian Roughley, John D. Heintz, Mark Richards, Michael Feathers, Mike Mangino, Nathaniel Schutta, Neal Ford, Raju Gandhi, Scott Davis, and Stuart Halloway. They have influenced this book in a number of good ways. Any errors you find in this book are entirely mine.

Special thanks to Scott Leberknight; he is one of the most thorough reviewers I've ever met. His comments were detailed and insightful, and he took the time to run every single piece of code in the book. He was kind enough to take a second pass at some of the areas I needed another pair of eyes on.

What can an author of a book on a programming language ask for that's better than having the author of the language review the book? I sincerely thank Martin Odersky for his invaluable comments, corrections, and suggestions.

The book you're reading is well-polished, copyedited, refined, and refactored. There is one person who braved to read and edit the words as they flowed through my fingers. And that he did, with only the latency that the Internet imposed between us. He showed me how someone could be hard on you and at the same time be motivating. I promised to write another book if he promised to edit it, and here we are. I thank Daniel Steinberg from the bottom of my heart.

My special thanks to the Pragmatic Programmers, Andy Hunt and Dave Thomas, for taking on this book project and supporting it to completion. Thank you for providing such an agile environment and the high standards you've set. It is a pleasure to write again for you. Thanks to Janet Furlow, Kim Wimpsett, Steve Peter, and the entire Pragmatic Bookshelf team for their assistance in creating this book.

I'd like to thank Dustin Whitney, Jonathan Smith, Josh McDonald, Fred Jason, Vladimir Kelman, and Jeff Sack for their encouragement on the discussion form for this book (see Appendix A, on page 207) and email communications. I also thank the readers of this book in the beta form and for their valuable comments and feedback. Thanks to Daniel Glauser, David Bailey, Kai Virkki, Leif Jantzen, Ludovic Kuty, Morris Jones, Peter Olsen, and Renaud Florquin for reporting errors in the beta book.

Thanks to Jay Zimmerman, director of NFJS Conference series (http://www.nofluffjuststuff.com), for providing me with an opportunity to present ideas and topics that have helped shape my books. Thanks to the geeks—speakers and attendees at conferences—I have had the opportunity to interact with. You guys are a source of inspiration, and I learn a great deal from you all.

I concurrently thank Martin Odersky and the Scala community for their effort in developing this wonderful language.

Writing this book would've been impossible without the enormous support, patience, and encouragement from my wife, Kavitha, and my sons, Karthik and Krupakar. This book started with Krupa asking "Daddy, what is Scala?" and finished with Karthik saying "I'm going to learn Scala this summer," with my wife keeping a steady flow of junk food, caffeinated beverages, and inquisitive questions in between. The following fully functional Scala code is for them: ("thank you! " * 3) foreach print.

Chapter 2

Getting Started

Let's get started writing Scala code. In this chapter, you'll install Scala and ensure everything is working well on your system.

2.1 Downloading Scala

Getting started with Scala is really easy. First, download the most recent stable version of Scala—just visit http://www.scala-lang.org, and click the "Download Scala" link. Download the appropriate version for the platform you're on. You will find the current release on the top.[1] For example, for Mac OS X, I downloaded scala-2.7.4.final.tar.gz. For Windows Vista, I downloaded scala-2.7.4.final.zip. If you're interested in the Scala API or the source code, you'll need to download additional files.

The examples in this book were tested against version 2.7.4 of Scala. If you are a bleeding-edge type, a stable version will not satisfy you. You will need the latest drop of the evolving language implementation. Scroll down the download page to the "Release Candidate" section, and download the latest release candidate version suitable for your platform. Alternately, if you need the absolutely latest and are willing to risk running into issues, you may instead pick the nightly build.

No matter which version you choose, you'll also need the JDK 1.4 or newer.[2] I recommend at least Java 5 so you can enjoy the latest Java language features in Scala. Take a moment to check which version of Java is installed and active on your system.

---

1. If for some reason you are looking for an older release, you can find it in the "Previous Releases" section.
2. See http://java.sun.com/javase/downloads/index.jsp.

2.2 Installing Scala

Let's get Scala installed. I'll assume you have downloaded the Scala 2.7.4 binary distribution and have verified your Java installation (Section 2.1, *Downloading Scala*, on the previous page).

Installing Scala on Windows

Unzip the distribution file—I right-clicked scala-2.7.4.final.zip in Windows Explorer and selected "Extract Here." Move the extracted directory to the appropriate location. For example, on my system, I moved scala-2.7.4.final to the C:\programs\scala directory.[3]

There is one more step. You'll need to set up the path to the Scala bin directory. To do this, go to the Control Panel, and open the "System" application. Navigate to "Advanced system settings," select "Advanced," and then select "Environment Variables."[4] Modify the *path* variable to include the Scala bin directory. For example, on my machine I added C:\programs\scala\scala-2.7.4.final\bin to the path. Remember to separate the directories in your path using a semicolon (;).

Let's make sure the setup went as expected. Close any open command-line windows because changes to the environment variables won't take effect until you reopen the windows. In a new command-line window, type scala -version, and make sure it reports the right version of Scala you just installed. You're all set to use Scala!

Installing Scala on Unix-like Systems

You have a couple of options if you want to install Scala on your Unix-like system. On Mac OS X, you can use MacPorts to install it using the command sudo port install scala.

Alternately, unzip the distribution file: gunzip scala-2.7.4.final.tar.gz. Then untar the file using tar -xf scala-2.7.4.final.tar. Move the unbundled directory to an appropriate location. For example, on my system, I copied scala-2.7.4.final to the /opt/scala directory.

There is one more step: setting up the path to the Scala bin directory.

---

3. I recommend you choose a path name with no whitespace in it, since path names with whitespace often cause trouble.
4. For Windows versions other than Vista, follow the appropriate steps to change environment variables.

Depending on the shell you use, edit the appropriate profile files. You most likely know what to edit—if you need help figuring out what to edit, refer to appropriate documentation for your shell, or consult someone who knows. I use bash, so I edited the ~/.bash_profile file. In that file, I added /opt/scala/scala-2.7.4.final/bin to the path environment variable.

Let's make sure the setup went as expected. Close any open terminal windows because changes to the environment variables won't take effect until you reopen the windows.[5] In a new terminal window, type scala -version, and make sure it reports the right version of Scala you just installed. You're all set to use Scala!

2.3 Take Scala for a Ride

The quickest way to try Scala is to use the command-line shell scala. It allows you to play with little Scala code snippets. This is a very useful tool to quickly try some new code while you are writing applications. On the command line (in a terminal window or command prompt), type scala. You should see an introductory message followed by a prompt:

```
>scala
Welcome to Scala version 2.7.4.final (Java HotSpot(TM) Client VM, Java 1.5.0_16).
Type in expressions to have them evaluated.
Type :help for more information.

scala>
```

At the prompt, type val number = 6, and hit Return. The Scala shell responds like this to indicate that it inferred the variable number to be an Int based on what we assigned to it (6):

```
scala> val number = 6
number: Int = 6

scala>
```

Now try entering number = 7, and Scala will respond with this error:

```
scala> number = 7
<console>:5: error: reassignment to val
       number = 7
              ^

scala>
```

---

5. Technically, we can source our profile file, but opening a new window is less trouble.

Scala tells us that we can't reassign the constant number. In the console, however, we can redefine constants and variables. So, we can now type val number = 7, and Scala will quietly accept it:

```
scala> val number = 7
number: Int = 7

scala>
```

Redefining constants and variables within the same scope is possible only in the interactive shell, and not in real Scala code or script—this flexibility makes it easier to experiment within the shell.

Try typing val list = List(1, 2, 3), and notice how Scala infers the type of list and reports list: List[Int] = List(1, 2, 3). At any time, if you're not sure what an expression will be inferred as, you can quickly try it in the shell.

You can use the up arrow to bring back commands you typed previously. It even can bring back commands from a previous invocation of the shell. While typing a line of command, you can press Ctrl+A to go to the beginning of the line or Ctrl+E to go to the end of the line.

The shell tries to execute what you type as soon as you hit the Return key. If you type something incomplete and press Return, for example in the middle of writing a method definition, the shell will allow you to complete the definition by prompting with a vertical bar (|). For example, here I define a method isPalindrome() on two lines, then call the method twice, and finally view the results:

```
scala> def isPalindrome(str: String) =
     | str == str.reverse.toString()
isPalindrome: (String)Boolean

scala> isPalindrome("mom")
res1: Boolean = true

scala> isPalindrome("dude")
res2: Boolean = false

scala>
```

When you are done with the shell, simply type :quit or exit to exit the shell. In addition to using the shell, we can send short statements or expressions to Scala on the command line using the -e (execute argument) option:

GettingStarted/RunScalaOnCommandLine.cmd

```
scala -e "println(\"Hello \"+args(0)+\", \"+args(1))" Buddy "Welcome to Scala"
```

Scala will respond with the following message:

```
Hello Buddy, Welcome to Scala
```

We used () instead of [] to index the args variable—this is a Scala idiom we will talk about later.

If you have Scala code in a file, you can load that into the shell using the :load option. For example, to load a filename script.scala, type within the shell :load script.scala. This option is useful to load and experiment with prewritten functions and classes.

2.4 Scala on the Command Line

Although the shell and the -e option are convenient ways to experiment with small pieces of code, you will soon want to upgrade to executing Scala code saved in files. The scala command can do that for you. It works in interactive mode if you don't provide any arguments, and it runs in batch mode if you provide a filename. The file may be a script file or an object file (an object file is a compiler-generated .class). By default, you can let the tool guess which type of file you're providing. Alternately, you can tell it to treat the file as a script file or as an object file using a -howtorun option. Finally, to send Java properties, you can use the -Dproperty=value format.

Suppose we have a file named HelloWorld.scala:

GettingStarted/HelloWorld.scala

```
println("Hello World, Welcome to Scala")
```

We can execute the script with the command scala HelloWorld.scala like this:

```
> scala HelloWorld.scala
Hello World, Welcome to Scala
>
```

We can follow the filename with any arguments we want to send to the program.

The ability to write Scala code into a file and run it as a script is quite convenient. You can use this to write code related to system maintenance or administrative tasks, for example, and run them from the command line or your favorite IDE without taking the extra step to compile.

The scala tool compiles your script into bytecode in memory and executes it. It rolls the code into the traditional main() method of a Main class. So, when you run the script, you're running the main() method of this Main class. If you want to view the bytecode generated, use the -savecompiled option before the filename, and the tool will save it to a JAR file.

2.5 Running Scala Code as a Script

As you begin to use Scala for writing scripts, you will find it easier to simply run the Scala file like you run a shell script.

Running as a Script on Unix-like Systems

On Unix-like systems, you can do that by setting a shell preamble. Here is an example:

GettingStarted/Script.scala

```
#!/usr/bin/env scala
!#
println("Hello " + args(0))
```

Make sure the file Script.scala has executable permission by typing chmod +x Script.scala. Then to run it, simply type ./Script.scala Buddy on the command line—Buddy is the argument that is passed to the script. Here's the output from the previous call:

```
Hello Buddy
```

Running as a Script on Windows

You can configure Windows to invoke Scala when you run a .scala file. To do that, within Windows Explorer, simply double-click a Scala script file with the .scala extension. Windows will complain that it can't open the file and will ask you to select a program from a list of installed programs. Browse to the location where Scala is installed, and select scala.bat. Now you can run the program by simply double-clicking it in Windows Explorer, or you can run it from the command prompt without prefixing with the command .scala. When you double-click the program within Windows Explorer, you will notice that a window pops up, displays the result of execution, and quickly shuts down. If you want to keep that window open, you can point the file to a .bat file that will run Scala and pause. To do this, right-click the Scala program, select "Open With...," and browse to and select the .bat file.

Here is an example:

GettingStarted/RunScala.bat

```
echo off
cls
call scala %1
pause
```

If you double-click HelloWorld.scala and automatically run the previous .bat file, you should see this:

```
C:\Windows\system32\cmd.exe
Hello World, Welcome to Scala
Press any key to continue . . .
```

2.6 Scala from an IDE

As Java developers, you most likely use an IDE to develop applications. If you're using Eclipse, IntelliJ IDEA, or NetBeans, you can use the Scala plug-ins for those IDEs (covered in Appendix A, on page 207). These IDEs allow you to enjoy with Scala the same facilities you're used to when editing and working with Java. You can use syntax highlighting, code completion, debugging, proper indentation, and so on, to name a few. Furthermore, you can mix and reference Scala and Java code in the same project.

To install the Scala plug-in for Eclipse, follow the instructions at http://www.scala-lang.org/node/94.

2.7 Compiling Scala

Here's how to write a class and compile it using the scalac compiler. In the following example, we define an object named Sample. (As you'll learn soon, Scala does not support static methods, so in order to write the static main() method, you need to define an object—a Singleton class.)

GettingStarted/Sample.scala

```
object Sample {
  def main(args: Array[String]) =  println("Hello Scala")
}
```

We can compile it using the command scalac Sample.scala. We can run it either using the scala tool or using the java command. To use the scala tool, simply type scala Sample. To use the java tool, we need to specify the classpath for scala-library.jar. Here's an example of compiling with the scalac tool and running the program first with the scala tool and then with the java tool on my Mac:

```
> scalac Sample.scala
> scala Sample
Hello Scala
> java -classpath /opt/scala/scala-2.7.4.final/lib/scala-library.jar:. Sample
Hello Scala
>
```

On Windows, you'd set the classpath to the location of the scala-library.jar file. As an example, on my Vista machine, I set it to C:\programs\scala\ scala-2.7.4.final\lib\scala-library.jar;.

In this chapter, we installed Scala and took it for a short drive. You are now all set to get into the nuts and bolts of Scala programming.

Chapter 3

Getting Up to Speed in Scala

Scala lets you build on your Java skills. In this chapter, we'll start on familiar ground—with Java code—and then move toward Scala. Scala is similar to Java in several ways and yet different in so many other ways. Scala favors pure object orientation, but it maps types to Java types where possible. Scala supports Java-like imperative coding style and at the same time supports a functional style. Crank up your favorite editor; we are ready to start on a tour through Scala.

3.1 Scala as Concise Java

Scala has very high code density—you type less to achieve more. Let's start with an example of Java code:

ScalaForTheJavaEyes/Greetings.java

```java
//Java code
public class Greetings {
  public static void main(String[] args) {
    for(int i = 1; i < 4; i++) {
      System.out.print(i + ",");
    }

    System.out.println("Scala Rocks!!!");
  }
}
```

Here's the output:

```
1,2,3,Scala Rocks!!!
```

Scala makes quite a few things in the previous code optional. First, it does not care whether we use semicolons. Second, there is no real

---

val vs. var

You can define a variable using either a val or a var. The variables defined using val are immutable and can't be changed after initialization. Those defined using var, however, are mutable and can be changed any number of times.

The immutability applies to the variable and not the instance to which the variable refers. For example, if we write val buffer = new StringBuffer(), we can't change what buffer refers to. However, we can modify the instance of StringBuffer using methods like append().

On the other hand, if we define an instance of String using val str = "hello", we can't modify the instance as well because String itself is immutable. You can make an instance of a class immutable by defining all of its fields using val and providing only the methods that let you read, and not modify, the state of the instance.

In Scala, you should prefer using val over var as much as possible since that promotes immutability and functional style.

---

benefit for the code to live within the class Greetings in a simple example like this, so we can get rid of that. Third, there's no need to specify the type of the variable i. Scala is smart enough to *infer* that i is an integer. Finally, Scala lets us use println without typing System.out.println. Here is the previous code simplified to Scala:

ScalaForTheJavaEyes/Greetings.scala

```scala
for (i <- 1 to 3) {
  print(i + ",")
}

println("Scala Rocks!!!")
```

To run the previous Scala script, type scala Greetings.scala, or run it from within your IDE.

You should see this output:

```
1,2,3,Scala Rocks!!!
```

The Scala loop structure is pretty lightweight. You simply mention that the values of the index i goes from 1 to 3. The left of the arrow (<-) defines a val, not a var (see the sidebar on the current page), and its right side is a generator expression. On each iteration, a new val is created and initialized with a consecutive element from the generated values.

The range that was generated in the previous code included both the lower bound (1) and the upper bound (3). You can exclude the upper bound from the range via the until() method instead of the to() method:

`ScalaForTheJavaEyes/GreetingsExclusiveUpper.scala`

```
for (i <- 1 until 3) {
  print(i + ",")
}

println("Scala Rocks!!!")
```

You'll see this output:

```
1,2,Scala Rocks!!!
```

Yes, you heard right. I did refer to to() as a *method*. to() and until() are actually methods on RichInt,[1] the type to which Int, which is the inferred type of variable i, is implicitly converted to. They return an instance of Range. So, calling 1 to 3 is equivalent to 1.to(3), but the former is more elegant. We'll discuss more about this charming feature in the sidebar on the next page.

In the previous example, it appears that we've reassigned i as we iterated through the loop. However, i is not a var; it is a val. Each time through the loop we're creating a different val named i. Note that we can't inadvertently change the value of i within the loop because i is immutable. Quietly, we've already taken a step toward functional style here.

We can also perform the loop in a more functional style using foreach():

`ScalaForTheJavaEyes/GreetingsForEach.scala`

```
(1 to 3).foreach(i => print(i + ","))

println("Scala Rocks!!!")
```

Here's the output:

```
1,2,3,Scala Rocks!!!
```

---

1. We'll discuss rich wrappers in Section 3.2, *Scala Classes for Java Primitives*, on the following page.

> ### The Dot and Parentheses Are Optional
>
> Scala allows you to drop both the dot and the parentheses if a method takes either zero or one parameter. If a method takes more than one parameter, you must use the parentheses, but the dot is still optional. You already saw benefits of this: a + b is really a.+(b), and 1 to 3 is really 1.to(3).
>
> You can take advantage of this lightweight syntax to create code that reads naturally. For example, assume we have a turn() method defined on a class Car:
>
> ```
> def turn(direction: String) //...
> ```
>
> We can call the previous method in a lightweight syntax as follows:
>
> ```
> car turn "right"
> ```
>
> Enjoy the optional dot and parentheses to reduce code clutter.

The previous example is concise, and there are no assignments. We used the foreach() method of the Range class. This method accepts a function value as a parameter. So, within the parentheses, we're providing a body of code that takes one argument, named in this example as i. The => separates the parameter list on the left from the implementation on the right.

3.2 Scala Classes for Java Primitives

Java presents a split view of the world—there are objects, and then there are primitives such as int, double, and so on. Scala treats everything as objects.

Java treats primitives differently from objects. Since Java 5, autoboxing allows you to send primitives to methods that expect objects. However, Java doesn't let you call a method on a primitive like this: 2.toString().

On the other hand, Scala treats everything as objects. This means you can call methods on literals, just like you can call methods on objects. In the following code, we create an instance of Scala's Int and send it to the ensureCapacity() method of java.util.ArrayList, which expects a Java primitive int.

ScalaForTheJavaEyes/ScalaInt.scala

```
class ScalaInt {
  def playWithInt() {
    val capacity : Int = 10
    val list = new java.util.ArrayList[String]
    list.ensureCapacity(capacity)
  }
}
```

In the previous code,[2] Scala quietly treated Scala.Int as the primitive Java int. The result is no performance loss at runtime for type conversions.

There is similar magic that allows you to call methods like to() on Int, as in 1.to(3) or 1 to 3. When Scala determines that Int can't handle your request, Scala quietly applies the intWrapper() method to convert[3] the Int to scala.runtime.RichInt and then invokes the to() method on it.

Classes like RichInt, RichDouble, RichBoolean, and so on, are called *rich wrapper* classes. They provide convenience methods that can be used for classes in Scala that represent the Java primitive types and String.

3.3 Tuples and Multiple Assignments

Suppose we have a function that returns multiple values. For example, let's return a person's first name, last name, and email address. One way to write it in Java is to return an instance of a PersonInfo class that holds the appropriate fields for data we'd like to return. Alternately, we can return a String[] or ArrayList containing these values and iterate over the result to fetch the values. There is a simpler way to do this in Scala. Scala supports tuples and multiple assignments.

A *tuple* is an immutable object sequence created as comma-separated values. For example, the following represents a tuple with three objects: ("Venkat", "Subramaniam", "venkats@agiledeveloper.com").

---

2. We could have defined val capacity = 10 and let Scala infer the type, but we specified it explicitly to illustrate the compatibility with Java int.

3. We will discuss implicit type conversions in Section 7.5, *Implicit Type Conversions*, on page 91.

We can assign the elements of a tuple into multiple vars or vals in parallel, as shown in this example:

ScalaForTheJavaEyes/MultipleAssignment.scala

```
def getPersonInfo(primaryKey : Int) = {
  // Assume primaryKey is used to fetch a person's info...
  // Here response is hard-coded
  ("Venkat", "Subramaniam", "venkats@agiledeveloper.com")
}

val (firstName, lastName, emailAddress) = getPersonInfo(1)

println("First Name is " + firstName)
println("Last Name is " + lastName)
println("Email Address is " + emailAddress)
```

Here's the output from executing this code:

```
First Name is Venkat
Last Name is Subramaniam
Email Address is venkats@agiledeveloper.com
```

What if you try to assign the result of the method to fewer variables or to more variables? Scala will keep an eye out for you and report an error if that happens. This error reporting is at compile time, assuming you're compiling your Scala code and not running it as a script. For example, in the following example, we're assigning the result of the method call to fewer variables than in the tuple:

ScalaForTheJavaEyes/MultipleAssignment2.scala

```
def getPersonInfo(primaryKey : Int) = {
  ("Venkat", "Subramaniam", "venkats@agiledeveloper.com")
}

val (firstName, lastName) = getPersonInfo(1)
```

Scala will report this error:

```
(fragment of MultipleAssignment2.scala):5: error:
  constructor cannot be instantiated to expected type;
 found    : (T1, T2)
 required: (java.lang.String, java.lang.String, java.lang.String)
val (firstName, lastName) = getPersonInfo(1)
    ^
...
```

Instead of assigning the values, you can also access individual elements of a tuple. For example, if we execute val info = getPersonInfo(1), then we can access the first element using the syntax info._1, the second element using info._2, and so on.

Tuples are useful not only for multiple assignments. They're useful to pass a list of data values as messages between actors in concurrent programming (and their immutable nature comes in handy here). Their concise syntax helps keep the code on the message sender side very concise. On the receiving side, you can use pattern matching to concisely receive and process the message, as you'll see in Section 9.3, *Matching Tuples and Lists*, on page 111.

3.4 Strings and Multiline Raw Strings

String in Scala is nothing but java.lang.String. You can use String just like the ways you do in Java. However, Scala does provide a few additional conveniences when working with String.

Scala can automatically convert a String to scala.runtime.RichString—this allows you to seamlessly apply some convenience methods like capitalize(), lines(), and reverse.[4]

If you need to create a string that runs multiple lines, it is really simple in Scala. Simply place the multiple lines of strings within three double quotes ("""..."""). That's Scala's support for here documents, or *heredocs*. Here, we create a string that runs three lines long:

`ScalaForTheJavaEyes/MultiLine.scala`

```
val str = """"In his famous inaugural speech, John F. Kennedy said
        "And so, my fellow Americans: ask not what your country can do
        for you-ask what you can do for your country." He then proceeded
        to speak to the citizens of the World..."""
println(str)
```

The output is as follows:

```
In his famous inaugural speech, John F. Kennedy said
        "And so, my fellow Americans: ask not what your country can do
        for you-ask what you can do for your country." He then proceeded
        to speak to the citizens of the World...
```

Scala lets you embed double quotes within your strings. Scala took the content within triple double quotes as is, so this is called a *raw string* in Scala. In fact, Scala took the string too literally; we wouldn't want

---

4. This seamless conversion, however, sometimes may catch you by surprise. For example, "mom".reverse == "mom" evaluates false, since we end up comparing an instance of RichString with an instance of String. "mom".reverse.toString == "mom", however, results in the desired result of true.

those indentations in the code to be carried into the string. We can use the convenience method stripMargin() of RichString like this:

`ScalaForTheJavaEyes/MultiLine2.scala`

```
val str = """"In his famous inaugural speech, John F. Kennedy said
        |"And so, my fellow Americans: ask not what your country can do
        |for you-ask what you can do for your country." He then proceeded
        |to speak to the citizens of the World...""".stripMargin
println(str)
```

stripMargin() removes all blanks or control characters before the leading pipe (|). If the pipe symbol appears anywhere else other than the leading position on each line, it's retained. If for some reason that symbol is sacred to you, you can use a variation of the stripMargin() method that accepts another margin character of your choice. You'll see this output for the previous code:

```
In his famous inaugural speech, John F. Kennedy said
"And so, my fellow Americans: ask not what your country can do
for you-ask what you can do for your country." He then proceeded
to speak to the citizens of the World...
```

You will find raw strings very useful when creating regular expressions. It's easier to type and to read """\d2:\d2""" than "\\d2:\\d2".

3.5 Sensible Defaults

Scala has some defaults that make the code concise and easier to read and write. Here are a few of these features:

- It has support for scripts. Not all code needs to be within a class. If a script is sufficient for your needs, you can put the executable code directly in a file without the clutter of an unnecessary class.

- return is optional. The last expression evaluated is automatically returned from method calls, assuming it matches with the return type declared for the method. Not having to put that explicit return makes your code concise, especially when passing closures as method parameters.

- Semicolons (;) are optional. You don't have to end each statement with a semicolon,[5] and this reduces noise in the code. If you want to place multiple statements in the same line, you can use semicolons to separate them. Scala also smartly figures out whether

---

5. See Section 3.7, *Semicolon Is Semi-optional*, on page 38.

a statement is not complete and allows you to continue on the
following line.

- Classes and methods are public by default, so you don't explicitly
use the keyword public.

- Scala provides lightweight syntax to create JavaBeans—it takes
less code to create variables and final properties (see Section 4.1,
Creating Classes, on page 45).

- You are not forced to catch exceptions you don't care about (see
Section 13.1, *Exception Handling*, on page 179), which reduces the
code size and also avoids improper exception handling.

In addition, by default Scala imports two packages, the scala.Predef
object, and their respective classes and members. You can refer to
classes from these preimported packages simply by using their class
names. Scala imports, in the following order, everything:

- java.lang

- scala

- scala.Predef

The inclusion of java.lang allows you to use common Java types in
scripts without any imports. So, you can use String, for example, without
prefixing with the package name java.lang or importing it.

You can also use Scala types easily since everything in package scala is
imported.

The Predef object contains types, implicit conversions, and methods
that are commonly used in Scala. So, since it is imported by default,
you are able to use those methods and conversions without any prefix
or import. They become so convenient that you will begin to believe that
they are part of the language, when they are actually part of the Scala
library.

The object Predef also provides aliases to things like scala.collection.
immutable.Set and scala.collection.immutable.Map. So, when you refer to
Set or Map, for instance, you are referring to their definitions in Predef,
which in turn refers to their definitions in the scala.collection.immutable
package.

3.6 Operator Overloading

Technically, Scala has no operators, but when I say "operator overloading," I mean overloading symbols like +, +-, and so on. In Scala, these are actually method names. Operators take advantage of Scala's lenient method invocation syntax—Scala does not require a dot (.) between the object reference and method name.

These two features give the illusion of operator overloading. So, when you call ref1 + ref2, you're actually writing ref1.+(ref2), and you're invoking the +() method on ref1. Let's look at an example of providing the + operator on a Complex class, a class that represents complex numbers:[6]

ScalaForTheJavaEyes/Complex.scala

```
class Complex(val real: Int, val imaginary: Int) {
  def +(operand: Complex) : Complex = {
    new Complex(real + operand.real, imaginary + operand.imaginary)
  }

  override def toString() : String = {
    real + (if (imaginary < 0) "" else "+") + imaginary + "i"
  }
}

val c1 = new Complex(1, 2)
val c2 = new Complex(2, -3)
val sum = c1 + c2
println("(" + c1 + ") + (" + c2 + ") = " + sum)
```

If you execute the previous code, you'll see this:

```
(1+2i) + (2-3i) = 3-1i
```

In the first statement, we created a class named Complex and defined a constructor that takes two parameters. We've used Scala's expressive syntax to create a class, as we'll see in Section 4.1, *Creating Classes*, on page 45.

Within the + method, we created a new instance of the Complex class. The real part and the imaginary part of the result is the sum of the real and imaginary parts of the two operands, respectively. The statement c1 + c2 resulted in a call to the +() method on c1 with c2 as an argument to the method call, that is, c1.+(c2).

---

6. Complex numbers have a real part and an imaginary part, and they're useful in computing complex equations that involve the square root of negative numbers.

We discussed Scala's simple and elegant support for operator overloading. However, the fact that Scala does not have operators is probably hurting your head a little. You may be wondering about operator precedence. Since Scala does not have operators, it can't define precedence on operators, right? Fear not, because 24 - 2 + 3 * 6 is 40 in both Java and Scala. Scala does not define precedence on operators. It defines precedence on methods.

The first character of methods is used to determine their priority.[7] If two characters with same priority appear in an expression, then the operator on the left takes higher priority. Here is the priority of the first letter listed from low to high:[8]

```
all letters
|
^
&
< >
= !
:
+ -
* / %
all other special characters
```

Let's look at an example of operator/method precedence. In the following code, we have defined both an add method and a multiply method on Complex:

ScalaForTheJavaEyes/Complex2.scala

```scala
class Complex(val real: Int, val imaginary: Int) {
  def +(operand: Complex) : Complex = {
    println("Calling +")
    new Complex(real + operand.real, imaginary + operand.imaginary)
  }

  def *(operand: Complex) : Complex = {
    println("Calling *")
    new Complex(real * operand.real - imaginary * operand.imaginary,
        real * operand.imaginary + imaginary * operand.real)
  }
  override def toString() : String = {
    real + (if (imaginary < 0) "" else "+") + imaginary + "i"
  }
}
```

---

7. Scala transposes the parameters of a method call if the method name ends with a colon (:); see Section 8.4, *Method Name Convention*, on page 103.
8. See "Scala Language Reference" in Appendix A, on page 207.

```
val c1 = new Complex(1, 4)
val c2 = new Complex(2, -3)
val c3 = new Complex(2, 2)
println(c1 + c2 * c3)
```

We are calling +() first on the left before calling *(), but since *() takes precedence, it is executed first, as you can see here:

```
Calling *
Calling +
11+2i
```

3.7 Scala Surprises for the Java Eyes

As you start to appreciate Scala's design elegance and conciseness, you should be aware of some Scala nuances—take the time to learn these to avoid surprises.

Result of Assignment

The result of the assignment operation ($a = b$) in Scala is a Unit. In Java, the result of the assignment is the value of a, so multiple assignments like $a = b = c$; can appear in series in Java, but not so in Scala. Since the result of assignment is a Unit, assigning that result to another variable will result in a type mismatch. Take a look at the following example:

> ScalaForTheJavaEyes/SerialAssignments.scala

```
var a, b, c = 1

a = b = c
```

When we attempt to execute the previous code, we'll get this compilation error:

```
(fragment of SerialAssignments.scala):3: error: type mismatch;
 found   : Unit
 required: Int
a = b = c
      ^
one error found
!!!
discarding <script preamble>
```

As much as Scala provides operator overloading, this behavior is at the least a minor annoyance.

Scala's ==

Java handles == differently for primitive types vs. objects. For primitive types, == means value-based comparison, whereas for objects it's identity-based comparison. So, if a and b are int, then a == b results in true if both the variables have equal values. However, if they're references to objects, the result is true only if both references are pointing to the same instance, that is, the same identity. Java's equals() method provides value-based comparison for objects, provided it is overridden correctly by the appropriate class.

Scala's handling of == is different from Java; however, it is consistent across all types. In Scala, == represents value-based comparison, no matter what the type is. This is ensured by implementing ==() as a final in the class Any (the class from which all types in Scala derive). This implementation uses the good old equals() method.

So, if you want to provide your own implementation of equality for your class, override the equals() method.[9] You can use a concise == instead of the equals() method for value-based comparison. If you want to perform the identity-based comparison on references, you can use the eq() method. Here is an example:

ScalaForTheJavaEyes/Equality.scala

```
val str1 = "hello"
val str2 = "hello"
val str3 = new String("hello")

println(str1 == str2) // Equivalent to Java's str1.equals(str2)
println(str1 eq str2) // Equivalent to Java's str1 == str2
println(str1 == str3)
println(str1 eq str3)
```

str1 and str2 are referring to the same instance of String, because Java interned the second "hello". However, str3 is referring to another newly created instance of String. All three references are pointing to objects that hold equal values (hello). str1 and str2 are equal in identity and so are also equal in value. However, str1 and str3 are equal only in value, but not in identity. The following output illustrates the semantics of the == and eq methods/operators used in the previous code:

```
true
true
true
false
```

Scala's handling of == is consistent for all types and avoids the common confusion of using == in Java. However, you must be aware of this departure from the Java semantics to avoid any surprises.

---

9. This is easier said than done. It is difficult to implement equals() in an inheritance hierarchy, as discussed in Joshua Bloch's *Effective Java* [Blo08].

Semicolon Is Semi-optional

Scala is lenient when it comes to statement termination—semicolons (;) are optional, and that reduces noise in code. You can place a semicolon at the end of a statement, particularly if you want to place multiple statements on the same line. Be careful, though. Placing multiple statements on the same line may reduce readability, as in the following: val sample = new Sample; println(sample).

Scala infers a semicolon if your statement does not end with an infix notation (like +, *, or .) or is not within parentheses or square brackets. It also infers a semicolon at the end of a statement if the next statement starts with something that can start a statement.

Scala, however, demands a semicolon in front of a {. The effect of not placing it may surprise you. Let's look at an example:

```
ScalaForTheJavaEyes/OptionalSemicolon.scala
val list1 = new java.util.ArrayList[Int];
{
  println("Created list1")
}

val list2 = new java.util.ArrayList[Int]
{
  println("Created list2")
}

println(list1.getClass())
println(list2.getClass())
```

That gives this output:

```
Created list1
Created list2
class java.util.ArrayList
class Main$$anon$2$$anon$1
```

We placed a semicolon when we defined list1. So, the { that followed it started a new code block. However, since we did not place a semicolon when we defined list2, Scala assumes we are creating an anonymous inner class that derives from ArrayList[Int]. So, list2 is referring to an instance of this anonymous inner class and not a direct instance of ArrayList[Int]. So, if your intent is to start a new code block after creating an instance, place a semicolon.

Java programmers are used to placing semicolons. Should you continue to use semicolons in Scala? In Java you had no choice. Scala gives you the freedom, and I recommend that you make use of it. The code is concise and less noisy without those semicolons. By dropping them, you can begin to enjoy an elegant lightweight syntax. Reserve the use of semicolon for cases like the previous when you have to resolve potential ambiguity.

Default Access Modifier

Scala's access modifier is different from Java:

- Java defaults to package internal visibility if you don't specify any access modifier. Scala, on the other hand, defaults to public.
- Java provides an all-or-nothing proposition. Either it's visible to all classes in the current package or it's not visible to any. Scala gives you a fine-grained control over visibility.
- Java's protected is generous. It includes derived classes in any package plus any class in the current package. Scala's protected is akin to C++ and C#—only derived classes can access it. However, you can also ask Scala for quite a liberal and flexible interpretation of protected.
- Finally, Java encapsulation is at the class level. You can access the private fields and methods of any object of your class from within an instance method. This is the default in Scala as well; however, you can restrict it to the current instance, like what Ruby provides.

Let's explore these variations from Java using some examples.

Default Access Modifier and How to Change It

By default, Scala treats classes, fields, and methods as public if you don't use an access modifier (Section 4.2, *Defining Fields, Methods, and Constructors*, on page 46). Also, you can quite easily make the primary constructor private (Section 4.5, *Stand-Alone and Companion Objects*, on page 52). If you want to make a member private or protected, simply mark it with the respective keyword like this:

ScalaForTheJavaEyes/Access.scala

```
class Microwave {
  def start() = println("started")
  def stop() = println("stopped")
  private def turnTable() = println("turning table")
}

val microwave = new Microwave
microwave.start()
microwave.turnTable() //ERROR
```

In the previous code, we have defined the methods start() and stop() as public. We can access those two methods on any instance of Microwave. On the other hand, we've defined turnTable() explicitly as private. We can't access that method from outside the class. If we try, as in the previous example, we will get this error:

```
(fragment of Access.scala):9: error:
  method turnTable cannot be accessed in this.Microwave
microwave.turnTable() //ERROR
          ^
one error found
!!!
discarding <script preamble>
```

Leave out any access modifier for public fields and methods. For other members, make the access as restrictive as you want by explicitly placing the access modifier.

Scala's Protected

In Scala, protected makes the decorated members visible to the class and its derived classes only. Other classes that belong to the package can't access these members. Furthermore, the derived class can access the protected members only on its own type. Let's examine these with an example:

ScalaForTheJavaEyes/Protected.scala

```
Line 1    package automobiles
    -
    -     class Vehicle {
    -       protected def checkEngine() {}
    5     }
    -
    -     class Car extends Vehicle {
    -       def start() { checkEngine() /*OK*/ }
    -       def tow(car: Car) {
    10        car.checkEngine() //OK
    -       }
    -       def tow(vehicle: Vehicle) {
    -         vehicle.checkEngine() //ERROR
    -       }
    15    }
    -
    -     class GasStation {
    -       def fillGas(vehicle: Vehicle) {
    -         vehicle.checkEngine() //ERROR
    20      }
    -     }
```

When we compile the previous code, we will get the following errors:

```
Protected.scala:13: error: method checkEngine cannot be accessed in
    automobiles.Vehicle
      vehicle.checkEngine() //ERROR
                 ^
Protected.scala:19: error: method checkEngine cannot be accessed in
    automobiles.Vehicle
      vehicle.checkEngine() //ERROR
                 ^
two errors found
```

In the previous code, checkEngine() of Vehicle is decorated as a protected method. Scala allows us to access that method from within an instance method (start()) of the derived class Car. We were also allowed to access it on an instance of Car from within an instance method (tow()) of Car. However, Scala does not allow us to access that method on an instance of Vehicle from within Car and also from within another arbitrary class (GasStation), which belongs to the same package as Vehicle. This behavior is different from how Java treats protected access. Scala is a lot more stringent about protecting the access to protected members.

Fine-Grained Access Control

On one hand, Scala is more restrictive than Java in how it treats the protected modifier. On the other hand, it gives you a far greater flexibility and also fine-grained control over setting access visibility. You can specify additional parameters for private and protected modifiers. So, instead of simply decorating a member with private, you can decorate it as private[AccessQualifier], where AccessQualifier may be this (meaning instance-only visibility) or any enclosing class name or package name. Read it as, "Treat this member as private for all classes, except for the current class, its companion object,[10] plus the class and companion object of the enclosing class whose name is given as the AccessQualifier, if the AccessQualifier is a class name." If the AccessQualifier is instead an enclosing package name, then the member is accessible within any class nested under the mentioned package. If the AccessQualifier is this, then the access to the member is restricted to the instance.

---

10. We will discuss companion objects in Chapter 4, *Classes in Scala*, on page 45.

Let's look at an example of the fine-grained access control:

```
ScalaForTheJavaEyes/FineGrainedAccessControl.scala
```

```scala
Line 1  package society  {

          package professional {
            class Executive {
     5        private[professional] var workDetails = null
              private[society] var friends = null
              private[this] var secrets = null

              def help(another : Executive) {
    10          println(another.workDetails)
                println(another.secrets) //ERROR
              }
            }
          }
    15
          package social {
            class Acquaintance {
              def socialize(person: professional.Executive) {
                println(person.friends) // OK
    20          println(person.workDetails) // ERROR
              }
            }
          }
        }
```

When we compile the previous code, we will get the following error:

```
FineGrainedAccessControl.scala:11: error: value secrets is not a member of
   society.professional.Executive
        println(another.secrets) //ERROR
                        ^
FineGrainedAccessControl.scala:20: error: variable workDetails cannot be
   accessed in society.professional.Executive
        println(person.workDetails) // ERROR
                       ^
two errors found
```

First observe how Scala allows you to define nested packages. Just like
C++ and C# namespaces, Scala allows you to nest a package within
another. So, you can follow the Java style to define packages (using
dots, as in package society.professional;) or the nested C++ or C# names-
pace style. If you decide to place multiple small classes belonging to a
hierarchy of packages in one file (again a departure from Java), you will
find the latter style convenient.

In the previous code, we gave visibility for the private field workDetails of Executive to any class within the enclosing package professional. However, we gave visibility for the private field friends to any class within the enclosing package society. Scala thus allows the class Acquaintance, which is located in the package society, to access the field friends but not the field workDetails.

The default visibility of private is class level—from an instance method of a class you can access the members decorated as private on any instance of the same class. However, Scala also allows you to decorate private and protected with this. For instance, in the previous example, since secret is decorated private[this], it is accessible only on the implicit object within instance methods (this)—you can't access it on other instances. Similarly, a field annotated with protected[this] is accessible from within an instance method of a derived class but only on the current instance.

Avoid Explicit return

In Java you use return to return results from methods. That's not a good practice in Scala. When Scala sees a return, it bails out of that method. At the least, it affects Scala's ability to infer the return type.

`ScalaForTheJavaEyes/AvoidExplitReturn.scala`

```
def check1() = true

def check2() : Boolean = return true
println(check1)
println(check2)
```

In the previous code, we had to explicitly provide the return type for the method that used the return; we'll get a compilation error if we don't. It is better to avoid using an explicit return statement. I prefer to let the compiler infer the return type, as in the method check1().

In this chapter, you took a quick drive through Scala from the perspective of Java programmers. You saw ways in which Scala is similar to Java and how, at the same time, it sets itself apart. While you are being drawn toward the strength of Scala, this chapter should prepare you to embark with full force. In the next chapter, you will see how Scala supports the OO paradigm.

Chapter 4

Classes in Scala

In this chapter, you'll create classes in Scala. You'll start by converting a simple Java class to a Scala class, and then you'll take a deeper dive into the differences. Constructors may look a little funny to you because Scala code tends to be more concise than Java code.

Also, even though Scala is a pure object-oriented language, it still has to support Java's not-so-pure OO concepts like static methods. Scala handles these concepts in a fairly interesting way using companion objects. Companion objects are singletons that accompany a class. These are very common in Scala. For instance, Actor is a companion object for the Actor class that you will use quite frequently when doing concurrent programming.

4.1 Creating Classes

Let's start with a Java example for creating a class that follows the bean convention of exposing its properties:

ScalaForTheJavaEyes/Car.java

```java
//Java example
public class Car {
  private final int year;
  private int miles;

  public Car(int yearOfMake) { year = yearOfMake; }

  public int getYear() { return year; }
  public int getMiles() { return miles; }

  public void drive(int distance) {
    miles += Math.abs(distance);
  }
}
```

In the previous code, the class Car has two properties, called year and miles, and the corresponding getter methods, called getYear() and get-Miles(). The drive() method allows us to manipulate the miles property, while the constructor initializes the final field year. So, we have a couple of properties, as well as methods to initialize and manipulate them.

Here's Scala's way of accomplishing the same thing:

ScalaForTheJavaEyes/Car.scala
```scala
class Car(val year: Int) {
 private var milesDriven: Int = 0

 def miles() = milesDriven

 def drive(distance: Int) {
  milesDriven += Math.abs(distance)
 }
}
```

In the Java version, we explicitly defined the field and method for the property year and wrote an explicit constructor. In Scala, the parameter to the class took care of defining that field and writing the accessor method. Here is how we would use the previous Scala class:

ScalaForTheJavaEyes/Car.scala
```scala
val car = new Car(2009)
println("Car made in year " + car.year)
println("Miles driven " + car.miles)
println("Drive for 10 miles")
car.drive(10)
println("Miles driven " + car.miles)
```

And here's the result:

```
Car made in year 2009
Miles driven 0
Drive for 10 miles
Miles driven 10
```

4.2 Defining Fields, Methods, and Constructors

Scala rolls the primary constructor into the class definition and provides a concise way to define fields and corresponding methods. Let's understand this with a few examples.

Let's start with the following Scala class definition:

ScalaForTheJavaEyes/CreditCard.scala

```scala
class CreditCard(val number: Int, var creditLimit: Int)
```

That's it. That's a full definition of a class. If you don't have anything to add to the class definition, you don't need the curly braces ({}). The previous code gave us quite a few things. Compile the previous code using scalac, and run javap -private CreditCard to see what the compiler generated for us:

```
Compiled from "CreditCard.scala"
public class CreditCard extends java.lang.Object implements scala.ScalaObject{
    private int creditLimit;
    private final int number;
    public CreditCard(int, int);
    public void creditLimit_$eq(int);
    public int creditLimit();
    public int number();
    public int $tag()         throws java.rmi.RemoteException;
}
```

First, Scala automatically made the class public—everything in Scala that you don't mark private or protected defaults to public.

We declared number as a val, so Scala defined number as a private final field and created a public method number() to help us fetch that value. Since we declared creditLimit as a var, Scala defined a private field named creditLimit and gave us a public getter and setter for it.[1]

If we don't declare a parameter as a val or var, then Scala creates a private field and a private getter and setter for it. However, that parameter is not accessible from outside the class.

Any expression or executable statement you put into the class definition is actually executed as part of the primary constructor. Let's take a look at an example:

ScalaForTheJavaEyes/Sample.scala

```scala
class Sample {
  println("You are constructing an instance of Sample")
}

new Sample
```

---

[1]. The default generated getters and setters do not follow the JavaBean conventions. Later in this section we'll see how to control that.

The output shows that when we create an instance of the class Sample, as part of the constructor execution our print statement is executed:

```
You are constructing an instance of Sample
```

In addition to the parameters we have provided in the primary constructor, we can define other fields, methods, and zero or more auxiliary constructors. In the following code, the this() method is our auxiliary constructor. We are also defining the variable position and overriding the toString():

ScalaForTheJavaEyes/Person.scala

```scala
class Person(val firstName: String, val lastName: String) {
  private var position: String = _

  println("Creating " + toString())

  def this (firstName: String, lastName: String, positionHeld: String) {
    this (firstName, lastName)
    position = positionHeld
  }

  override def toString() : String = {
    firstName + " " + lastName + " holds " + position + " position "
  }
}

val john = new Person("John", "Smith", "Analyst")
println(john)
val bill = new Person("Bill", "Walker")
println(bill)
```

Here's the output from the previous code:

```
Creating John Smith holds null position
John Smith holds Analyst position
Creating Bill Walker holds null position
Bill Walker holds null position
```

Our primary constructor[2] takes the two parameters firstName and last-Name. The auxiliary constructor takes three parameters—the first two are the same as the primary constructor, and the third is positionHeld. From within the auxiliary constructor, we're calling the primary constructor to initialize the name-related fields. The first statement within an auxiliary constructor is required to be a call to either the primary constructor or another auxiliary constructor.

---

2. You can easily make the primary constructor private if you want; see Section 4.5, *Stand-Alone and Companion Objects*, on page 52.

Scala treats fields specially. Any var defined within a class is mapped to a private field declaration followed by the definition of corresponding accessor methods—getter and setter. The access privilege you mark on the field is used for accessor methods. So, in the previous example, when we declared the field private var position: String = _, Scala created the following:

```
private java.lang.String position;
private void position_$eq(java.lang.String);
private java.lang.String position();
```

So, Scala creates a special method position() for the getter and position_=() for the setter.

In the previous definition of position, you could have set the initial value to null. Instead, we used an underscore (_). In this context, the _ stands for the default value for the type—so, for Int, it is 0. For Double, it is 0.0. For a reference type, it is null, and so on. Scala provides the convenience of initializing var to its default value using the underscore. This convenience is not available for val, however, since it can't be modified; therefore, we're required to give it the appropriate value when we initialize.

If you prefer the traditional JavaBean-like getter and setter, you simply can mark your field with the scala.reflect.BeanProperty annotation. For this you use the Scala syntax for annotation, which is similar to the Java annotation syntax. For example, the following annotation instructs Scala to create the accessor methods getAge() and setAge():

```
@scala.reflect.BeanProperty var age: Int = _
```

4.3 Extending a Class

Extending from a base class in Scala is similar to extending in Java except for two restrictions: method overriding requires the override keyword, and only the primary constructor can pass parameters to the base constructor.

Scala insists that you use the keyword override when you override a method. The override annotation was introduced in Java 5 but is still optional in Java. By requiring that keyword, Scala will help minimize the problems because of typos in method names. You can either avoid accidentally overriding a method you did not intend to or avoid writing a new method when your intent was to override a base method.

In Scala, auxiliary constructors have to call either the primary constructor or another auxiliary constructor. You can pass parameters to a base constructor only from the primary constructor. In Scala, the primary constructor is the gateway to initialize an instance of a class, and the interaction with the base class for initialization is controlled through this.

Here's an example of extending from a base class:

`ScalaForTheJavaEyes/Vehicle.scala`

```
class Vehicle(val id: Int, val year: Int) {
  override def toString() : String = "ID: " + id + " Year: " + year
}

class Car(override val id: Int, override val year: Int,
  var fuelLevel: Int) extends Vehicle(id, year) {
  override def toString() : String = super.toString() + " Fuel Level: " + fuelLevel
}

val car = new Car(1, 2009, 100)
println(car)
```

Take a look at the output:

```
ID: 1 Year: 2009 Fuel Level: 100
```

When we extend the class Vehicle, we pass the parameters to the base class. The parameters we send should match one of the constructors of the base class. Since the properties id and year in Car are derived from Vehicle, we indicate that by using the keyword override in the primary constructor parameter of Car. Finally, since we're overriding the toString() method of java.lang.Object, in Vehicle and Car we prefix the definitions of toString() with override as well.

4.4 Singleton Object

A singleton (see *Design Patterns: Elements of Reusable Object-Oriented Software* [GHJV95] by Gamma et al.) is a class that has only one instance. We use singletons to represent objects that act as a central point of contact for certain operations such as database access, object factories, and so on. Creating singleton objects in Scala is very simple. You create them using the keyword object instead of class. Since you can't instantiate a singleton object, you can't pass parameters to the primary constructor.

Here is an example of a singleton—MarkerFactory:

`ScalaForTheJavaEyes/Singleton.scala`

```scala
class Marker(val color: String) {
  println("Creating " + this)

  override def toString() : String = "marker color " + color
}

object MarkerFactory {
  private val markers = Map(
    "red" -> new Marker("red"),
    "blue" -> new Marker("blue"),
    "green" -> new Marker("green")
  )

  def getMarker(color: String) =
    if (markers.contains(color)) markers(color) else null
}

println(MarkerFactory getMarker "blue")
println(MarkerFactory getMarker "blue")
println(MarkerFactory getMarker "red")
println(MarkerFactory getMarker "red")
println(MarkerFactory getMarker "yellow")
```

Here's the result:

```
Creating marker color red
Creating marker color blue
Creating marker color green
marker color blue
marker color blue
marker color red
marker color red
null
```

Assume we have a class Marker that represents color markers for primary colors. The MarkerFactory is a singleton that allows us to reuse precreated instances of Marker for the three primary colors. A call to getMarker() will return the appropriate Marker instance for the given primary color. If the argument is not a primary color, it returns a null. We can access the singleton (the only instance) of MarkerFactory by its name. Once you define a singleton, its name represents the single instance of the singleton object. You can pass around the singleton to functions like you pass around instances in general.

There is one problem in the previous code, however. We can directly create an instance of Marker without going through the MarkerFactory. We will solve this problem in the next section.

4.5 Stand-Alone and Companion Objects

The MarkerFactory we just saw is an example of a *stand-alone* object. It is not automatically connected to any class, even though we have used it to manage instances of Marker.

Scala also allows you to create a singleton that is connected to a class. Such a singleton will share the same name as a class name and is called a *companion object*. The corresponding class is called a *companion class*. In the previous example, we want to regulate the creation of Marker instances. In Scala, classes and their companion objects have no boundaries—they can access the private fields and methods of each other. Also, in Scala, you can mark a constructor private. Here is a rewrite of the Marker example using a companion object:

ScalaForTheJavaEyes/Marker.scala

```scala
class Marker private (val color: String) {
  println("Creating " + this)

  override def toString() : String = "marker color " + color
}

object Marker {
  private val markers = Map(
    "red" -> new Marker("red"),
    "blue" -> new Marker("blue"),
    "green" -> new Marker("green")
  )

  def getMarker(color: String) =
    if (markers.contains(color)) markers(color) else null
}
```

Here is some example code that uses the modified class:

ScalaForTheJavaEyes/UseMarker.scala

```scala
println(Marker getMarker "blue")
println(Marker getMarker "blue")
println(Marker getMarker "red")
println(Marker getMarker "red")
```

Here's the output:

```
Creating marker color red
Creating marker color blue
Creating marker color green
marker color blue
marker color blue
marker color red
marker color red
```

The constructor of Marker is marked private; however, the companion object can access it. So, we're able to instantiate instances of Marker from within the companion object. If we try to create an instance of Marker outside the class or the companion object, we'll get an error.

Each class may have an optional companion object that you write in the same file as their companion classes. Companion objects are common in Scala and provide class-level convenience methods. They also serve as a nice workaround for the lack of static members in Scala, as you will see next.

4.6 static in Scala

Scala does not have static fields and methods. Allowing static fields and methods would break the fully object-oriented model that Scala supports. However, Scala fully supports class-level operations and properties. This is where companion objects come in.

Let's revisit the previous Marker example. It would be nice to get the primary colors from the Marker. However, that is not a valid operation on a specific instance; it's a class-level operation. In other words, you would have written it as a static method in Java. In Scala, that method will reside in the companion object:

`ScalaForTheJavaEyes/Static.scala`

```scala
class Marker private (val color: String) {
  override def toString() : String = "marker color " + color
}

object Marker {
  private val markers = Map(
    "red" -> new Marker("red"),
    "blue" -> new Marker("blue"),
    "green" -> new Marker("green")
  )

  def primaryColors = "red, green, blue"

  def apply(color: String) = if (markers.contains(color)) markers(color) else null
}

println("Primary colors are : " + Marker.primaryColors)
println(Marker("blue"))
println(Marker("red"))
```

This is the output:

```
Primary colors are : red, green, blue
marker color blue
marker color red
```

We wrote the method primaryColors() in the companion object (the parentheses in the method definition are optional if the method takes no parameters). We can call it on the Marker companion object like we'd call static methods on classes in Java.

The companion object also provides another benefit, the ability to create instances of the companion class without the need for the new keyword. The special apply() method, for which Scala provides syntax sugar, does this trick. In the previous example, when we invoke Marker("blue"), we're actually calling Marker.apply("blue"). This is a lightweight syntax to create or get instances.[3]

You were introduced to Scala's support of the OO paradigm in this chapter. You're now ready to enjoy Scala's conciseness and pure object orientation. In the next chapter, we will discuss one of the key features of Scala—*static* typing.

---

3. Also, Scala does not require () when using new if your constructor takes no parameters—so you can use new Sample instead of new Sample().

Chapter 5

Sensible Typing

Static typing, or compile-time type checking, helps you define and verify interface contracts at compile time. Scala, unlike some of the other statically typed languages, does not expect you to provide redundant type information. You don't have to specify a type in most cases, and you certainly don't have to repeat it. At the same time, Scala will infer the type and verify proper usage of references at compile time. Let's explore this with an example:

SensibleTyping/Typing.scala

```
var year: Int = 2009
var anotherYear = 2009
var greet = "Hello there"
var builder = new StringBuilder("hello")

println(builder.getClass())
```

Here we defined a variable year explicitly as type Int. We also defined anotherYear as a variable but let Scala infer the type as Int based on what we assigned to that variable. Similarly, we let Scala infer the type of greet as String and builder as StringBuilder. We can query the reference builder to find what type it's referring to. If you attempt to assign some other type of value or instance to any of these variables, you'll get a compilation error. Scala's type inference is low ceremony[1] and has no learning curve; you simply have to undo some Java practices.

Scala's static typing helps you in two ways. First, the compile-time type checking can give you confidence that the compiled code *meets* certain

---

1. See "Essence vs. Ceremony" in Appendix A, on page 207.

expectations.[2] Second, it helps you to *express* the expectations on your API in a compiler-verifiable format.

In this chapter, you'll learn about Scala's sensible static typing and type inference. You'll also look at three special types in Scala: Any, Nothing, and Option.

5.1 Collections and Type Inference

Scala will provide type inference and type safety for the Java Generics collections as well. The following is an example that uses an ArrayList. The first declaration uses explicit, but redundant, typing. The second declaration takes advantage of type inference.

As an aside, note that the underscore in the import statement is equivalent to the asterisks in Java. So when we type java.util._, we are importing all classes in the java.util package. If the underscore follows a class name instead of a package name, we are importing all members of the class—the equivalent of Java static import:

`SensibleTyping/Generics.scala`

```
import java.util._

var list1 : List[Int] = new ArrayList[Int]
var list2 = new ArrayList[Int]

list2 add 1
list2 add 2

var total = 0
for (val index <- 0 until list2.size()) {
  total += list2.get(index)
}

println("Total is " + total)
```

Here's the output:

```
Total is 3
```

---

2. As you'll see, this is not a substitute for good unit testing, but you can use the good compiler support as a first level of defense.

Scala is vigilant about the type of the object you instantiate. It prohibits conversions that may cause typing issues.[3] Here's an example of how Scala differs from Java when it comes to handling Generics:

`SensibleTyping/Generics2.scala`

```
import java.util._

var list1 = new ArrayList[Int]
var list2 = new ArrayList

list2 = list1 // Compilation Error
```

We created a reference, list1, that points to an instance of ArrayList[Int]. Then we created another reference, list2, that points to an instance of ArrayList with an unspecified parametric type. Behind the scenes, Scala actually created an instance of ArrayList[Nothing]. When we try to assign the first reference to the second, Scala gives us this compilation error.[4]

```
(fragment of Generics2.scala):6: error: type mismatch;
 found   : java.util.ArrayList[Int]
 required: java.util.ArrayList[Nothing]
list2 = list1 // Compilation Error
          ^
one error found
!!!
discarding <script preamble>
```

Nothing is a subclass of all classes in Scala. By treating the new ArrayList as an instance of ArrayList[Nothing], Scala rules out any possibility of adding an instance of any meaningful type to this collection. This is because you can't treat an instance of base as an instance of derived and Nothing is the bottom-most subclass.

So, how can you create a new ArrayList without specifying the type? One way is to use the type Any. You saw how Scala deals with an assignment when one collection holds objects of type Nothing, while the other does not. Scala, by default, insists the collection types on either side of assignment are the same (you'll see later in Section 5.7, *Variance of Parameterized Type*, on page 63 how you can alter this default behavior in Scala).

---

3. Of course, Scala has no control over conversions that happen in compiled Java or other language code that you call.
4. Equivalent Java code will compile with no errors but result in a runtime ClassCastException.

Here is an example using a collection of objects of type Any—Any is the base type of all types in Scala:

SensibleTyping/Generics3.scala

```
import java.util._

var list1 = new ArrayList[Int]
var list2 = new ArrayList[Any]

var ref1 : Int = 1
var ref2 : Any = null

ref2 = ref1 //OK

list2 = list1 // Compilation Error
```

This time list1 refers to an ArrayList[Int], while list2 refers to an ArrayList[Any]. We also created two other references, ref1 of type Int and ref2 of type Any. Scala has no qualms about letting us assign ref1 to ref2. So, it is equivalent to assigning an Integer reference to a reference of type Object. However, Scala doesn't allow, by default, assigning a collection of arbitrary type instances to a reference of a collection of Any instances (later we'll discuss covariance, which provides exceptions to this rule). You saw how Java Generics enjoy enhanced type safety in Scala.

You don't have to specify the type in order to benefit from Scala type checking. You can just rely on the type inference where it makes sense. The inference happens at compile time. So, you can be certain that the type checking takes effect right then when you compile the code.

Scala insists that a nonparameterized collection be a collection of Nothing and restricts assignment between types. These combine to enhance type safety at compile time—providing for a sensible, low-ceremony static typing.

In the previous examples, we used the Java collections. Scala also provides a wealth of collections, as you'll see in Chapter 8, *Using Collections*, on page 95.

5.2 The Any Type

Scala's Any type is a superclass of all types in Scala, graphically illustrated in the following diagram.

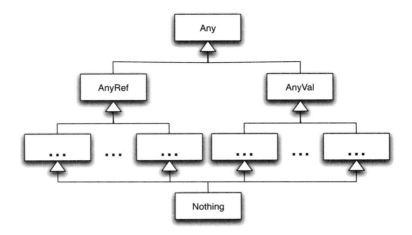

Any allows you to hold a common reference to objects of any type in Scala. Any is an abstract class with the following methods: !=(), ==(), asInstanceOf(), equals(), hashCode(), isInstanceOf(), and toString().

The direct descendants of Any are AnyVal and AnyRef. AnyVal serves as a base for all types in Scala that map over to the primitive types in Java—for example, Int, Double, and so on. On the other hand, AnyRef is the base for all reference types. Although AnyVal does not have any additional methods, AnyRef contains the methods of Java's Object such as notify(), wait(), and finalize().

AnyRef directly maps to the Java Object, so you can pretty much use it in Scala like you'd use Object in Java. On the other hand, you can't call all the methods of Object on a reference of Any or AnyVal, even though internally Scala treats them as Object references when compiled to bytecode. In other words, while AnyRef directly maps to Object, Any and AnyVal are type erased to Object much like type erasure of Generics parameterized types in Java.

5.3 More About Nothing

You can see why you'd need Any, but what is the purpose of Nothing?

Scala's type inference works hard to determine the type of expressions and functions. If the type inferred is too broad, it will not help type verification. At the same time, how do you infer the type of an expression or function if one branch returns, say, an Int and another branch throws an exception? In this case, it is more useful to infer the type as Int rather than a general Any. This means that the branch that throws the exception must be inferred to return an Int or a subtype of Int for it to be compatible. However, an exception may occur at any place, so not all those expressions can be inferred as Int. Scala helps type inference work smoothly with the type Nothing, which is a subtype of all types. Since it is a subtype of all types, it is substitutable for anything. Nothing is abstract, so you would not have a real instance of it anywhere at runtime. It is purely a helper for type inference purposes.

Let's explore this further with an example. Let's take a look at a method that throws an exception and see how Scala infers the type:

```
def madMethod() = { throw new IllegalArgumentException() }
```

```
println(getClass().getDeclaredMethod("madMethod", null).
  getReturnType().getName())
```

The method madMethod() simply throws an exception. Using reflection, we're querying the return type of this method with this result:[5]

```
scala.runtime.Nothing$
```

Scala infers the return type of an expression that throws an exception as Nothing. Scala's Nothing is actually quite something—it is a subtype of every other type. So, Nothing is substitutable for anything in Scala.

5.4 Option Type

Scala goes a step further in specifying nonexistence. When you perform pattern matching, for example, the result of the match may be an object, a list, a tuple, and so on, or it may be nonexistent. Returning a null quietly is problematic in two ways. First, the intent that you actually expect nonexistence of a result is not expressed explicitly. Second, there is no way to force the caller of your function to check for nonexistence (null). Scala wants you to clearly specify your intent that sometimes you do actually expect to give no result. Scala achieves this in a type-safe manner using the Option[T] type. Let's look at an example:

SensibleTyping/OptionExample.scala
```
def commentOnPractice(input: String) = {
  //rather than returning null
  if (input == "test") Some("good") else None
}
```

---

5. The $ symbol indicates an internal representation in Scala.

```
for (input <- Set("test", "hack")) {
  val comment = commentOnPractice(input)
  println("input " + input + " comment " +
    comment.getOrElse("Found no comments"))
}
```

Here, commentOnPractice() may return a comment (String) or may not
have any comments at all. This is represented as instances of Some[T]
and None, respectively. These two classes extend from the Option[T]
class. The output from the previous code is as follows:

```
input test comment good
input hack comment Found no comments
```

By making the type explicit as Option[String], Scala forces us to check
for the nonexistence of an instance. You're less likely to get NullPointerEx-
ception because of unchecked null references. By calling the getOrElse()
method on the returned Option[T], you can proactively indicate what to
do in case the result is nonexistent (None).

5.5 Method Return Type Inference

In addition to inferring the types of variables, Scala also tries to infer
the return type of methods. However, there is a catch. It depends on
how you define your method. If you define your method with an equals
sign (=), then Scala infers the return type. Otherwise, it assumes the
method is a void method. Let's look at an example:

`SensibleTyping/Methods.scala`

```
def printMethodInfo(methodName: String) {
  println("The return type of " + methodName + " is " +
    getClass().getDeclaredMethod(methodName, null).getReturnType().getName())
}

def method1() { 6 }
def method2() = { 6 }
def method3() = 6
def method4 : Double = 6

printMethodInfo("method1")
printMethodInfo("method2")
printMethodInfo("method3")
printMethodInfo("method4")
```

We've defined method1() like we normally define methods, by providing
a method name, a parameter list within parentheses, and the method
body within curly braces. Unfortunately, the way we're used to is not

a idiomatic way to define methods in Scala. We have used equals (=) to define the method method2(). The equal sign is the only difference between the two methods; however, that is significant in Scala. Scala infers method1() as a void method and method2() as returning an Int (Java's int). This is shown here:

```
The return type of method1 is void
The return type of method2 is int
The return type of method3 is int
The return type of method4 is double
```

If the method definition or body is small and can be condensed into a single expression, you can leave out the {}, as in the previous method3(). This can be useful for simple getters and setters that perform minimal checks.

You can also override the default type inference of Scala by providing the desired type, as in method4(). We have declared the return type of method4() as Double. We may also declare it as Unit, Short, Long, Float, and so on. We can choose any type that the result of the method execution is compatible with. If it is not—for example, if we declare the return type of method4() as String—Scala will give a type-mismatch compile-time error.

In general, it is better to use the = and let Scala infer the type of methods. You have one less thing to worry about, and you can let the well-built type inference do the job for you.

5.6 Passing Variable Arguments (Varargs)

If your method takes parameters, you need to specify the parameter names and their types:

```
def divide(op1: Double, op2: Double) = op1/op2
```

You can write a method that takes a variable number of arguments (*varargs*). However, only the trailing parameter can take variable number of arguments. Use the special symbol (*) after the type information, as in this max() method:

```
def max(values: Int*) = values.foldLeft(values(0)) { Math.max }
```

Scala treats the varargs parameter (values in the previous example) as an array, so we can iterate over it. We can invoke the method with a variable number of arguments by simply sending an arbitrary number of arguments:

```
println(max(2, 5, 3, 7, 1, 6))
```

Although we can send discrete arguments, we can't, however, send an array. Suppose we have defined an array like this:

```
val numbers = Array(2, 5, 3, 7, 1, 6)
```

The following code will result in an error:

```
println(max(numbers)) // type mismatch error
```

If we want to use the values in an array as variable arguments, we can explode the array into discrete values—use the series of symbols : _* for this purpose:

```
println(max(numbers: _*))
```

5.7 Variance of Parameterized Type

You have seen a lot of Scala idioms, but there is one final thing I want to introduce in this chapter. You may find this section a bit intense, but I am confident you can handle it. So, let's tighten our seat belts!

You saw how Scala prevents you from making assignments that may potentially lead to runtime failures. Specifically, it prevents the following code from compiling:

```
var arr1 = new Array[Int](3)
var arr2: Array[Any] = null

arr2 = arr1 // Compilation ERROR
```

The previous restriction is a good thing. Imagine if Scala—like Java—did not restrict that. Here is Java code that can get us into trouble:

ScalaIdioms/Trouble.java

```
Line 1  //Java code
   -    class Fruit {}
   -    class Banana extends Fruit {}
   -    class Apple extends Fruit {}
   5
   -    public class Trouble {
   -      public static void main(String[] args) {
   -        Banana[] basketOfBanana = new Banana[2];
   -        basketOfBanana[0] = new Banana();
  10
   -        Object[] basketOfFruits = basketOfBanana; // Trouble
   -        basketOfFruits[1] = new Apple();
   -
   -        for(Banana banana : basketOfBanana) {
  15          System.out.println(banana);
   -        }
   -      }
   -    }
```

The previous code will compile with no errors. However, when we run it, it will give us the following runtime error:

```
Exception in thread "main" java.lang.ArrayStoreException: Apple
        at Trouble.main(Trouble.java:12)
```

To be fair, Java does not allow the following:

```
//Java code
ArrayList<Integer> list = new ArrayList<Integer>();
ArrayList<Object> list2 = list; // Compilation error
```

However, it is easy to bypass this in Java like this:

```
ArrayList list3 = list;
```

The ability to send a collection of subclass instances to a collection of base class is called *covariance*. And the ability to send a collection of superclass instances to a collection of subclass is called *contravariance*. By default Scala does not allow either one of them.

Although the default behavior of Scala is good in general, there are genuine cases where you'd want to cautiously treat a collection of a derived type (say a collection of Dogs) as a collection of its base type (say a collection of pets). Consider the following example:

`Scalaldioms/PlayWithPets.scala`

```
class Pet(val name: String) {
  override def toString() = name
}

class Dog(override val name: String) extends Pet(name)

def workWithPets(pets: Array[Pet]) {}
```

We've defined two classes—a Dog that extends a class Pet. We have a method workWithPets() that accepts an array of Pets but really does nothing. Now, let's create an array of Dogs:

`Scalaldioms/PlayWithPets.scala`

```
val dogs = Array(new Dog("Rover"), new Dog("Comet"))
```

If we send the dogs to the previous method, we will get a compilation error:

```
workWithPets(dogs) // Compilation ERROR
```

Scala will complain when we call workWithPets()—we can't send an array of Dogs to a method that accepts an array of Pets. But, the method is benign, right? However, Scala does not know that, and it's trying to protect us. We have to tell Scala that it is OK to let this happen. Here's an example of how we can do that:

Scalaldioms/PlayWithPets.scala

```
def playWithPets[T <: Pet](pets: Array[T]) =
  println("Playing with pets: " + pets.mkString(", "))
```

We've defined the method playWithPets() with a special syntax. T <: Pet indicates that the class represented by T is derived from Pet. By using this syntax for the upper bound,[6] we're telling Scala that the parameterized type T of the parameter array must be at least an array of Pet but can be an array of any class derived from Pet. So, now we are allowed to make the following call:

Scalaldioms/PlayWithPets.scala

```
playWithPets(dogs)
```

Here's the corresponding output:

```
Playing with pets: Rover, Comet
```

If we try to send an array of Objects or an array of objects of some type that does not derive from Pets, we'll get a compilation error.

Now let's say we want to copy pets. We can write a method named copy() that accepts two parameters of type Array[Pet]. However, that will not help us send an array of Dogs. Furthermore, we can copy from an array of Dogs into an array of Pets. In other words, the receiving array can be a collection of supertypes of the class of the source array. What we need is a lower bound:

Scalaldioms/PlayWithPets.scala

```
def copyPets[S, D >: S](fromPets: Array[S], toPets: Array[D]) = { //...
}

val pets = new Array[Pet](10)
copyPets(dogs, pets)
```

We've constrained the destination array's parameterized type (D) to be a supertype of the source array's parameterized type (S). In other words, S (for a source type like Dog) sets the lower bounds for the type D (for a destination type like Dog or Pet)—it can be any type that is type S or its supertype.

---

6. If you visualize the object hierarchy, Pet defines the upper bound of type T, and T can be any type Pet or lower in the hierarchy.

In the previous two examples, we controlled the parameters of methods in the method definition. You can also control this behavior if you're the author of a collection—that is, if you assume that it is OK for a collection of derived to be treated as a collection of base. You can do this by marking your parameterized type as +T instead of T, as in the following example:

Scalaldioms/MyList.scala

```scala
class MyList[+T] //...

var list1 = new MyList[int]
var list2 : MyList[Any] = null

list2 = list1 // OK
```

Here, +T tells Scala to allow covariance; in other words, during type checking, it asks Scala to accept a type or its base type. So, we're able to assign a MyList[Int] to MyList[Any]. Remember, this was not possible for Array[Int]. However, this is possible for the functional list List implemented in the Scala library—we'll discuss these in Chapter 8, *Using Collections*, on page 95.

Similarly, you can ask Scala to support contravariance on your types using -T instead of T for parameterized types.

By default, the Scala compiler strictly enforces the variance. You saw how you can request lenience for covariance or contravariance. In any case, the Scala compiler will check for type soundness of variance annotation.

In this chapter, we discussed the static typing in Scala and its type inference. You saw how this makes the code concise. With the understanding of typing, type inference, and how to write methods, you're all set to learn and enjoy concepts that lead to more conciseness in the next chapter.

Chapter 6

Function Values and Closures

As the name implies, functions are first-class citizens in functional programming. You can pass functions to functions as parameters, return them from functions, and even nest functions within functions. These higher-order functions are called *function values*. Once you get the hang of them, you'll begin to structure your application around these function values as building blocks. You'll quickly realize that they lead to concise, reusable code. Closures are special forms of function values that close over or bound to variables defined in another scope or context. In this chapter, you'll learn how to use function values and closures in Scala.

6.1 Moving from Normal to Higher-Order Functions

How would we find the sum of values in a given range 1 to number in Java? We'd probably write a method like this:

```java
// Java code
public int sum(int number) {
  int result = 0;
  for(int i = 1; i <= number; i++) {
    result += i;
  }
  return result;
}
```

What if in addition we now need to count the number of even numbers and the number of odd numbers in that range? We could copy the previous method and change the body to do the new tasks. That's the best we can do with normal functions, but that's code duplication with poor reusability.

In Scala, we'll pass an anonymous function to the function that iterates over the range. So, we can pass different logic to achieve different tasks. Such functions that can take other functions as parameters are called *higher-order functions*. They reduce code duplication, increase reusability, and make your code concise as well. Let's see how to create them in Scala.

6.2 Function Values

In Scala, you can create functions within functions, assign them to references, and pass them around to other functions. Scala internally deals with these so-called function values by creating them as instances of special classes. So, in Scala, function values are really objects.

Let's rewrite our previous example in Scala using function values. Suppose we want to perform different operations (such as summing numbers or counting the number of even numbers) on a range of values.

We'll start by first extracting the common code, which is that code for looping over the range of values, into a method named totalResultOver-Range():

```scala
def totalResultOverRange(number: Int, codeBlock: Int => Int) : Int = {
  var result = 0
  for (i <- 1 to number) {
    result += codeBlock(i)
  }

  result
}
```

We've defined two parameters for the method totalResultOverRange(). The first one is an Int for the range of values to iterate over. The second one is special; it's a function value. The name of the parameter is codeBlock, and its type is a function that accepts an Int and returns an Int.[1] The result of the method totalResultOverRange() is itself an Int.

In the body of the totalResultOverRange() method we iterate over the range of values, and for each element we invoke the given function (codeBlock). The given function is expected to receive an Int, representing an element in the range, and return an Int as a partial result of computation on that element. The computation or operation itself is

---

1. You can think of a function as transforming input to output without having any side effects.

left to be defined by the caller of the method totalResultOverRange(). We total the partial results of calls to the given function value and return that total.

The previous code removed the duplication from the example in Section 6.1, *Moving from Normal to Higher-Order Functions*, on page 67. Here is how we'd call the method totalResultOverRange() to get the sum of values in the range:

```
println(totalResultOverRange(11, i => i))
```

We passed two arguments to the method. The first argument is the upper limit (11) of the range we want to iterate over. The second argument is actually an anonymous just-in-time function, that is, a function with no name but only an implementation. The implementation, in this example, simply returns the given parameter. The => separates the parameter list on the left from the implementation on the right. Scala was able to infer that the type of the parameter (i) is an Int from the parameter list of totalResultOverRange(). Scala will give us an error if the parameter's type or the result type does not match with what's expected.

Instead of finding the sum, if we'd like to count the even numbers in the range, we'd call the method like this:

```
println(totalResultOverRange(11, i => if (i % 2 == 0) 1 else 0))
```

If we'd like to count the odd numbers, we can call the method as follows:

```
println(totalResultOverRange(11, i => if (i % 2 != 0) 1 else 0))
```

Scala allows you to accept any number of parameters as function values, and they can be any parameter, not just the trailing parameter.

It was quite easy to make the code DRY[2] using function values. We gathered up the common code into a function, and the differences were rolled into arguments of method calls. Methods that accept function values are commonplace in the Scala library, as you'll see in Chapter 8, *Using Collections*, on page 95. Scala makes it easy to pass multiple parameters and define the types of arguments as well, if you desire, as you'll see soon.

---

2. See *The Pragmatic Programmer* [HT00] by Andy Hunt and David Thomas for details about the Don't Repeat Yourself (DRY) principle.

6.3 Function Values with Multiple Parameters

You can define and use function values with multiple parameters. Here is an example of a method inject() that passes the result of the operation on one element in an array of Int to the operation on the next element. It allows us to cascade or accumulate results from operations on each element.

```
def inject(arr: Array[Int], initial: Int, operation: (Int, Int) => Int) : Int = {
  var carryOver = initial
  arr.foreach(element => carryOver = operation(carryOver, element) )
  carryOver
}
```

The inject() method takes three parameters: an array of Int, an initial Int value to inject into the operation, and the operation itself as a function value. In the method we set a variable carryOver to the initial value. We loop through the elements of the given array using the foreach() method. This method accepts a function value as a parameter, which it invokes with each element in the array as an argument. In the function that we send as an argument to foreach(), we're invoking the given operation with two arguments: the carryOver value and the context element. We assign the result of the operation call to the variable carryOver so it can be passed as an argument in the subsequent call to the operation. When we're done calling the operation for each element in the array, we return the final value of carryOver.

Let's look at a couple of examples of using the previous inject() method. Here's how we would total the elements in the array:

```
val array = Array(2, 3, 5, 1, 6, 4)
val sum = inject(array, 0, (carryOver, elem) => carryOver + elem)
println("Sum of elements in array " + array.toString() + " is " + sum)
```

The first argument to the method inject() is an array whose elements we'd like to sum. The second argument is an initial value 0 for the sum. The third argument is the function that carries out the operation of totaling the elements, one at a time.

If instead of totaling the elements we'd like to find the maximum value, we can use the same inject() method:

```
val max = inject(array, Integer.MIN_VALUE,
    (carryOver, elem) => Math.max(carryOver, elem)
  )
println("Max of elements in array " + array.toString() + " is " + max)
```

Here's the output of executing the previous two calls to the inject()
method:

```
Sum of elements in array Array(2, 3, 5, 1, 6, 4) is 21
Max of elements in array Array(2, 3, 5, 1, 6, 4) is 6
```

If you'd like to navigate over elements in a collection and perform operations, you don't have to really roll out your own inject() method—I wrote it only for illustrative purpose. The Scala library already has this method built in. It is the foldLeft() method. It is also the method /:.[3] Here is an example of using it to get the sum and max of elements in an array:

```
val array = Array(2, 3, 5, 1, 6, 4)

val sum = (0 /: array) { (sum, elem) => sum + elem }
val max = (Integer.MIN_VALUE /: array) {
  (large, elem) => Math.max(large, elem) }

println("Sum of elements in array " + array.toString() + " is " + sum)
println("Max of elements in array " + array.toString() + " is " + max)
```

As an observant reader, you probably noticed the function value was placed inside curly braces instead of being sent as an argument to the function. That looks a lot better than sending those functions as arguments within parentheses. However, if we attempt the following on the inject() method, we will get an error:

FunctionValuesAndClosures/Inject3.scala

```
val sum = inject(array, 0) {(carryOver, elem) => carryOver + elem}
```

The previous code will result in the following error:

```
(fragment of Inject3.scala):11: error: wrong number of arguments for
  method inject: (Array[Int],Int,(Int, Int) => Int)Int
val sum = inject(array, 0) {(carryOver, elem) => carryOver + elem}
            ^
one error found
!!!
discarding <script preamble>
```

That was not quite what we'd like to see. Before you can get the same benefit of using the curly braces that the library method enjoyed, you have to learn one more concept—currying.

---

3. See Section 8.4, *Method Name Convention*, on page 103 to learn about methods with names that end of a colon (:).

6.4 Currying

Currying in Scala transforms a function that takes more than one parameter into a function that takes multiple parameter lists. If you're calling a function multiple times with the same set of arguments, you can reduce the noise and spice up your code by using currying.

Let's see how Scala provides support for currying. Instead of writing a method that takes one parameter list with multiple parameters, write it with multiple parameter lists with one parameter each (you may have more than one parameter in each list as well). That is, instead of def foo(a: Int, b: Int, c: Int) {}, write it as def foo(a: Int)(b: Int)(c: Int) {}. We can then call it as, for example, foo(1)(2)(3), foo(1){2}{3}, or even foo{1}{2}{3}.

Let's examine what goes on when you define a method with multiple parameter lists. Take a look at the following interactive Scala shell session:

```
scala> def foo(a: Int)(b: Int)(c:Int) {}
foo: (Int)(Int)(Int)Unit

scala> foo _
res1: (Int) => (Int) => (Int) => Unit = <function>

scala>
```

We first defined the function foo() we discussed previously. Then we called foo _ to create a partially applied function (see Section 6.8, *Partially Applied Functions*, on page 79), that is, a function with one or more parameters unbound. We could've assigned the created partially applied function to a variable but did not care to in this example. We're focused on the message from the interactive shell. It shows a series of three transformations. Each function in the chain takes one Int and returns a partially applied function. The last one, however, results in a Unit.

The creation of partially applied functions when you curry is Scala's internal business. From a practical point of view, they help you to pass function values with syntactic sugar. So, let's rewrite the inject() method from the previous section in the curried form:

FunctionValuesAndClosures/Inject4.scala

```
def inject(arr: Array[Int], initial: Int)(operation: (Int, Int) => Int) : Int = {
  var carryOver = initial
  arr.foreach(element => carryOver = operation(carryOver, element))
  carryOver
}
```

The multiple parameter lists are the only difference between the previous version and the earlier version of the inject() method. The first parameter list takes two parameters, and the second one takes one, the function value.

So, we don't have to send the function values as comma-separated parameters within parentheses anymore. We can use the much nicer curly bracket to call this method:

FunctionValuesAndClosures/Inject4.scala

```
val array = Array(2, 3, 5, 1, 6, 4)
val sum = inject(array, 0) { (carryOver, elem) => carryOver + elem }
println("Sum of elements in array " + array.toString() + " is " + sum)
```

6.5 Reusing Function Values

You saw how function values help create more reusable code and eliminate code duplication. But, embedding a method as an argument to another method doesn't encourage reuse of that code. You can, however, create references to function values and therefore reuse them as well. Let's look at an example.

Assume we have a class Equipment that expects us to provide a calculation routine for its simulation. We can send in the calculation as a function value to the constructor like this:

FunctionValuesAndClosures/Equipment.scala

```
class Equipment(val routine : Int => Int) {
  def simulate(input: Int) = {
    print("Running simulation...")
    routine(input)
  }
}
```

When we create instances of Equipment, we can pass in a function value as a parameter to the constructor.

FunctionValuesAndClosures/EquipmentUseNotDry.scala

```
val equipment1 = new Equipment({input => println("calc with " + input); input })
val equipment2 = new Equipment({input => println("calc with " + input); input })

equipment1.simulate(4)
equipment2.simulate(6)
```

Here's the output:

```
Running simulation...calc with 4
Running simulation...calc with 6
```

In the previous code, we want to use the same calculation code for both the Equipment instances. Unfortunately, that code is duplicated. The code is not DRY, and if we decide to change the calculation, we'd have to change both. It would be good to create that once and reuse it. We can assign the function value to a val and reuse it like this:

FunctionValuesAndClosures/EquipmentUseDry.scala

```
val calculator = { input : Int => println("calc with " + input); input }

val equipment1 = new Equipment(calculator)
val equipment2 = new Equipment(calculator)

equipment1.simulate(4)
equipment2.simulate(6)
```

The output from the previous code is shown here:

```
Running simulation...calc with 4
Running simulation...calc with 6
```

We stored the function value into a reference named calculator. Scala needed a little help with the type information when we defined this function value. In the earlier example, Scala inferred the input as Int based on the context of the call. However, since we're defining this function value as stand-alone, we had to tell Scala the type of the parameter. We then passed the name of the reference as an argument to the constructor in the two instances we created.

In the previous example, we created a reference calculator to a function value. This may feel more natural to you since you're used to defining references/variables within functions or methods. However, in Scala, you can define full functions within other functions. So, there is a more idiomatic way of achieving the previous goal of reuse. Scala makes it really easy to do the right thing. It allows you to pass in a normal function where a function value is expected.

FunctionValuesAndClosures/EquipmentUseDry2.scala

```
def calculator(input: Int) = { println("calc with " + input); input }

val equipment1 = new Equipment(calculator)
val equipment2 = new Equipment(calculator)

equipment1.simulate(4)
equipment2.simulate(6)
```

We created our calculation as a function and passed in the name of the function as an argument to the constructor when we created those two instances. Scala comfortably treated that as a reference to a function value within the Equipment.

You don't have to compromise on good design principles and code quality when programming in Scala. On the contrary, it promotes good practices, and you should strive to make use of that when coding in Scala.

6.6 Positional Notation for Parameters

Scala provides the notation _, the underscore, to represent parameters of a function value. You can use this if you plan to use that parameter only once in the function. Each time you use the underscore within a function, it represents a subsequent parameter. Let's look at an example now:

FunctionValuesAndClosures/Underscore.scala

```
val arr = Array(1, 2, 3, 4, 5)

println("Sum of all values in array is " +
  (0 /: arr) { (sum, elem) => sum + elem }
)
```

In the previous code, we're using the /: method to compute the sum of elements in the array. Since we're using sum and elem only once each, we can eliminate those names and write the code as follows:

FunctionValuesAndClosures/Underscore.scala

```
println("Sum of all values in array is " +
  (0 /: arr) { _ + _ }
)
```

The first occurrence of _ represents the value carried over in the invocation of the function, and the second represents elements in the array.[4] You may argue that code is terse and you lost readability—the names sum and elem were helpful to have. That is a valid point. So, you may want to use the _ in places where the code is concise without any loss of readability, like in the following example:

FunctionValuesAndClosures/Underscore.scala

```
val negativeNumberExists = arr.exists { _ < 0 }
println("Array has negative number? " + negativeNumberExists)
```

---

4. If Scala can't determine the type, it will complain. If that happens, we can either provide the type for _ or step back to using parameter names with type.

Where it makes sense, you can take this conciseness further. Assume we have a function that determines the maximum of two numbers. We want to use that function to determine the maximum among elements of an array. Let's start with how we'd simply use that with the /:() method:

```
def max2(a: Int, b: Int) : Int = if (a > b) a else b
var max = (Integer.MIN_VALUE /: arr) { (large, elem) => max2(large, elem) }
```

We are sending the pair of values (large and elem) to the max2() method to determine which of those two is larger. We use the result of that computation to eventually determine the largest element in the array. Use the _ to simplify this:

```
max = (Integer.MIN_VALUE /: arr) { max2(_, _) }
```

The _ represents not only a single parameter; it can represent the entire parameter list as well. So, we can modify the call to max2() as follows:

```
max = (Integer.MIN_VALUE /: arr) { max2 _ }
```

In the previous code, the _ represents the entire parameter list, that is, (parameter1, parameter2). If you are merely passing what you receive to an underlying method, you don't even need the ceremony of the _. We can further simplify the previous code:

```
max = (Integer.MIN_VALUE /: arr) { max2 }
```

As you can see, you can adjust the conciseness dial of Scala to the extent you're comfortable with. While you enjoy the benefit of conciseness, however, you need to make sure your code does not become cryptic—you have to strike that gentle balance.

6.7 Execute Around Method Pattern

As a Java programmer, you're familiar with the synchronized block. When you enter it, it obtains a monitor (lock) on the given object. That monitor is automatically released when you leave the synchronized block. The release happens even if the code within the block throws an unhandled exception. That kind of deterministic behavior is nice to have. Unfortunately, while Java provided that mechanism for synchronized, it did not provide a good way to implement that kind of behavior for your own code. You may try to achieve that using anonymous inner classes, but the code you end up with will scare the daylights out of you.

Fortunately, you can implement those constructs in Scala quite easily. Let's look at an example.

Assume we have a class named Resource that needs to start some transaction automatically and end the transaction deterministically as soon as we're done using the object. We can rely on the constructor to correctly start the transaction. It's the ending part that poses the challenge. This falls into the Execute Around Method pattern (see Kent Beck's *Smalltalk Best Practice Patterns* [Bec96]). We want to execute a pair of operations in tandem around an arbitrary set of operations on an object.

We can use function values to implement this pattern in Scala. Here is the code for the Resource class along with its companion object (see Section 4.5, *Stand-Alone and Companion Objects*, on page 52 for details on companion objects):

FunctionValuesAndClosures/Resource.scala

```scala
class Resource private() {
  println("Starting transaction...")

  private def cleanUp() { println("Ending transaction...") }

  def op1 = println("Operation 1")
  def op2 = println("Operation 2")
  def op3 = println("Operation 3")
}

object Resource {
  def use(codeBlock: Resource => Unit) {
    val resource = new Resource

    try {
      codeBlock(resource)
    }
    finally {
      resource.cleanUp()
    }
  }
}
```

We've marked the constructor of the Resource class private. So, we can't create an instance of this class outside the class and its companion object. This forces us to use the object in a certain way, thus guaranteeing automatic and deterministic behavior. The cleanUp() method is declared private as well. The print statements are placeholders for real transaction operations. The transaction starts when the constructor is called and ends when cleanUp() is implicitly called. The usable instance methods of the Resource class are methods like op1(), op2(), and so on.

In the companion object, we have a method named use() that accepts a function value as a parameter. The use() method creates an instance of Resource, and within the safeguard of the try and finally blocks, we send the instance to the given function value. In the finally block, we call the private instance method cleanUp() of the Resource. Pretty simple, eh? That's all it took to provide a deterministic call to necessary operations.

Now let's take a look at how we can use the Resource class. Here's some example code:

FunctionValuesAndClosures/UseResource.scala

```
Resource.use { resource =>
  resource.op1
  resource.op2
  resource.op3
  resource.op1
}
```

The output from the previous code is shown here:

```
Starting transaction...
Operation 1
Operation 2
Operation 3
Operation 1
Ending transaction...
```

We invoke the use() method of the Resource companion object and provide it with a code block. It sends to us an instance of Resource. By the time we get access to resource, the transaction has been started. We invoke the methods we desire (like op1(), op2(), ...) on the instance of Resource. When we're done, at the time we leave the code block, the cleanUp() method of the Resource is automatically called by the use() method.

A variation of the previous pattern is described as the Loan pattern (see Appendix A, on page 207). Use it if your intent is to deterministically dispose of nonmemory resources. The resource-intensive object is considered to be on loan to you, and you're expected to return it promptly.

Here is an example of how to use this pattern:

FunctionValuesAndClosures/WriteToFile.scala

```
import java.io._

def writeToFile(fileName: String)(codeBlock : PrintWriter => Unit) = {
  val writer = new PrintWriter(new File(fileName))
  try { codeBlock(writer) } finally { writer.close() }
}
```

Now we can use the function writeToFile() to write some content to a file:

FunctionValuesAndClosures/WriteToFile.scala

```
writeToFile("output.txt") { writer =>
  writer write "hello from Scala"
}
```

When we run the code, the contents of the file output.txt are as follows:

```
hello from Scala
```

As a user of the method writeToFile(), we don't have to worry about closing the file. The file is on loan to us to use within the code block. We can write to the PrintWriter instance given to us, and upon return from the block, the file is automatically closed by the method.

6.8 Partially Applied Functions

When you invoke a function, you're said to be applying the function to the arguments. If you pass all the expected arguments, you have fully applied it. If you send only a few arguments, then you get back a partially applied function. This gives you the convenience of binding some arguments and leaving the rest to be filled in later. Let's take a look at an example:

FunctionValuesAndClosures/Log.scala

```
import java.util.Date

def log(date: Date, message: String) {
  //...
  println(date + "----" + message)
}

val date = new Date
log(date, "message1")
log(date, "message2")
log(date, "message3")
```

In the previous code, the log() method takes two parameters: date and message. We want to invoke the method multiple times, with the same value for date but different values for message. We can eliminate the noise of passing the date to each call by partially applying that argument to the log() method.

In the next code sample, we first bind a value to the date parameter. We use the _ to leave the second parameter unbound. The result is a partially applied function that we've stored in the reference logWith-DateBound. We can now invoke this new method with only the unbound argument message:

FunctionValuesAndClosures/Log.scala

```
val logWithDateBound = log(new Date, _ : String)
logWithDateBound("message1")
logWithDateBound("message2")
logWithDateBound("message3")
```

When you create a partially applied function, Scala internally creates a new class with a special apply() method. When you invoke the partially applied function, you are actually invoking that apply method—see Section 8.1, *Common Scala Collections*, on page 95 for more details on the apply method. Scala makes extensive use of partially applied functions when pattern matching messages received from an actor, as you'll see in Chapter 10, *Concurrent Programming*, on page 125.

6.9 Closures

In the examples you've seen so far in this chapter, the variables and values used in the function values or code blocks were bound. You clearly knew what they were bound to, local variables or parameters. In addition, you can create code blocks with variables that are not bound. You will have to bind them before you can invoke the function; however, they could bind to, or close over, variables outside of their local scope and parameter list. That's why they're called *closures*.

Let's look at a variation of the totalResultOverRange() method you saw earlier in this chapter. The method loopThrough() in this example iterates over the elements from 1 to a given number:

FunctionValuesAndClosures/Closure.scala

```
def loopThrough(number: Int)(closure: Int => Unit) {
  for (i <- 1 to number) { closure(i) }
}
```

The loopThrough() method takes a code block as the second parameter, and for each element in the range of 1 through its first parameter, it calls the given code block. Let's define a code block to pass to this method:

FunctionValuesAndClosures/Closure.scala

```
var result = 0
val addIt = { value:Int => result += value }
```

In the previous code, we have defined a code block and assigned it to the variable named addIt. Within the code block, the variable value is bound to the parameter. However, the variable result is not defined within the block or its parameter list. This is actually bound to the variable result outside the code block. The code block stretches its hands and binds to a variable outside. Here's how we can use the code block in calls to the method loopThrough():

`FunctionValuesAndClosures/Closure.scala`

```scala
loopThrough(10) { addIt }
println("Total of values from 1 to 10 is " + result)

result = 0
loopThrough(5) { addIt }
println("Total of values from 1 to 5 is " + result)
```

When we pass the closure to the method loopThrough(), the value is bound to the parameter passed by loopThrough(), while result is bound to the variable in the context of the caller of loopThrough().

The binding did not get a copy of the variable's current value; it's actually bound to the variable itself. So, when we reset the value of result to 0, the closure sees this change as well. Furthermore, when the closure sets result, we see it in the main code. Here's another example of a closure bound to yet another variable product:

`FunctionValuesAndClosures/Closure.scala`

```scala
var product = 1
loopThrough(5) { product *= _ }
println("Product of values from 1 to 5 is " + product)
```

In this case, the _ refers to the parameter passed in by loopThrough(), and product is bound to the variable with that name in the caller of loopThrough().

Here's the output from the three calls to loopThrough():

```
Total of values from 1 to 10 is 55
Total of values from 1 to 5 is 15
Product of values from 1 to 5 is 120
```

In this chapter, you explored the concepts related to function values and saw how functions are first-class citizens in Scala. You can probably see the benefit of using these code blocks where you want to enhance the functionality of another function. You can use them in places where you want to specify a predicate, a query, or a constraint to the logic being implemented in a method. You can use them to alter the control flow of a method, for example, in iterating over a collection of values. You have learned in this chapter a valuable tool that you will use quite frequently in Scala, both in your own code and most commonly when using the Scala library. In the next chapter, you will walk through another interesting Scala idiom, traits.

Chapter 7

Traits and Type Conversions

Traits are like interfaces with a partial implementation. Traits provide a middle ground between single and multiple inheritance because you can mix them in or include them in other classes. This allows you to enhance a class with a set of features.

Single implementation inheritance forces you to model everything into a linear hierarchy. However, the real world is full of crosscutting concerns —concepts that cut across and affect abstractions that do not fall under the same class hierarchy. Security, logging, validation, transactions, resource allocation, and management are all examples of such cross-cutting concerns in a typical enterprise application. Scala's traits allow you to apply those concerns to arbitrary classes without the pain that arises from multiple implementation inheritance.

In this chapter, you'll learn Scala's support for abstraction and object models. Much of this will feel like magic. Scala's implicit conversion allows you to treat an instance of one class as an instance of another. This allows you to attach methods to an object without modifying the original class, by implicitly wrapping the instance in a façade. You'll use that trick to see how to create a DSL.

7.1 Traits

A *trait* is a behavior that can be mixed into or assimilated into a class hierarchy. Say we want to model a Friend. We can mix that into any class, Man, Woman, Dog, and so on, without having to inherit them all from a common base class.

Assume we've modeled a class Human and want to make it friendly. A friend is someone who listens. So, here is the listen method that we'd add to the Human class:

```
class Human(val name: String) {
  def listen() = println("Your friend " + name + " is listening")
}

class Man(override val name: String) extends Human(name)
class Woman(override val name: String) extends Human(name)
```

One disadvantage of the previous code is the friendly quality does not quite stand out and is merged into the Human class. Furthermore, a few weeks into development, we realize we forgot man's best friend. Dogs are great friends—they listen to us quietly when we have a lot to unload. But, how can we make a Dog a friend? We can't inherit a Dog from a Human for that purpose. The Java approach to solving this problem would be to create an interface Friend and have Human and Dog implement it. We're forced to provide different implementations in these two classes irrespective of whether the implementations are different.

This is where Scala's traits come in. A *trait* is like an interface with a partial implementation. The vals and vars you define and initialize in a trait get internally implemented in the classes that mix the trait in. Any vals and vars defined but not initialized are considered abstract, and the classes that mix in these traits are required to implement them. We can reimplement the Friend concept as a trait:

TraitsAndTypeConversions/Friend.scala

```
trait Friend {
  val name: String
  def listen() = println("Your friend " + name + " is listening")
}
```

Here we have defined Friend as a trait. It has a val named name that is treated as abstract. We also have the implementation of a listen() method. The actual definition or the implementation of name will be provided by the class that mixes in this trait. Let's look at ways to mix in the previous trait:

TraitsAndTypeConversions/Human.scala

```
class Human(val name: String) extends Friend
```

TraitsAndTypeConversions/Man.scala

```
class Man(override val name: String) extends Human(name)
```

```
TraitsAndTypeConversions/Woman.scala
```

```scala
class Woman(override val name: String) extends Human(name)
```

The class Human mixes in the Friend trait. If a class does not extend from any other class, then use the extends keyword to mix in the trait. The class Human and its derived classes Man and Woman simply use the implementation of the listen() method provided in the trait. We can override this implementation if we like, as we'll see soon.

You can mix in any number of traits. To mix in additional traits, use the keyword with. You will also use the keyword with to mix in your first trait if your class already extends from another class like the Dog in this next example. In addition to mixing in the trait, we have overridden its listen() method in Dog.

```
TraitsAndTypeConversions/Animal.scala
```

```scala
class Animal
```

```
TraitsAndTypeConversions/Dog.scala
```

```scala
class Dog(val name: String) extends Animal with Friend {
  //optionally override method here.
  override def listen = println(name + "'s listening quietly")
}
```

You can call the methods of a trait on the instances of classes that mix it in. You can also treat a reference to such classes as a reference of the trait:

```
TraitsAndTypeConversions/UseFriend.scala
```

```scala
val john = new Man("John")
val sara = new Woman("Sara")
val comet = new Dog("Comet")

john.listen
sara.listen
comet.listen

val mansBestFriend : Friend = comet
mansBestFriend.listen

def helpAsFriend(friend: Friend) = friend listen

helpAsFriend(sara)
helpAsFriend(comet)
```

The output from the previous code is shown here:

```
Your friend John is listening
Your friend Sara is listening
```

```
Comet's listening quietly
Comet's listening quietly
Your friend Sara is listening
Comet's listening quietly
```

Traits look similar to classes but have some significant differences. First, they require the mixed-in class to implement the uninitialized (abstract) variables and values declared in them. Second, their constructors cannot take any parameters. Traits are compiled into Java interfaces with corresponding implementation classes that hold any methods implemented in the traits.

Traits do not suffer from the method collision problem that generally arise from multiple inheritance. They avoid it by late binding with the method of the class that mixes them in. So, a call to super within a trait resolves to a method on another trait or the class that mixes it in, as you'll see soon.

7.2 Selective Mixins

In the previous example, we mixed the trait Friend into the Dog class. This allows us to treat *any* instance of the Dog class as a Friend; that is, all Dogs are Friends.

You can also mix in traits selectively at an instance level. This will allow you to treat a specific instance of a class as a trait. Let's look at an example:

TraitsAndTypeConversions/Cat.scala

```scala
class Cat(val name: String) extends Animal
```

Cat does not mix in the Friend trait, so we can't treat an instance of Cat as a Friend. Any attempts to do so, as you can see here, will result in compilation errors:

TraitsAndTypeConversions/UseCat.scala

```scala
def useFriend(friend: Friend) = friend listen

val alf = new Cat("Alf")
val friend : Friend = alf // ERROR

useFriend(alf) // ERROR
```

Here you can see the errors:

```
(fragment of UseCat.scala):4: error: type mismatch;
 found    : Cat
 required: Friend
val friend : Friend = alf // ERROR
                      ^
(fragment of UseCat.scala):6: error: type mismatch;
 found    : Cat
 required: Friend
useFriend(alf) // ERROR
          ^
two errors found
!!!
discarding <script preamble>
!!!
discarding <script preamble>
```

Scala, however, does offer help for cat lovers, and we can exclusively treat our special pet as a Friend if we want. When creating an instance, simply mark it using the with keyword:

TraitsAndTypeConversions/TreatCatAsFriend.scala

```scala
def useFriend(friend: Friend) = friend listen

val snowy = new Cat("Snowy") with Friend
val friend : Friend = snowy
friend.listen

useFriend(snowy)
```

Here's the output:

```
Your friend Snowy is listening
Your friend Snowy is listening
```

Scala gives you the flexibility to treat all the instances of a class as a trait or to select only the instances you want. The latter is especially useful if you want to apply traits to preexisting classes.

7.3 Decorating with Traits

You can use traits to decorate[1] objects with capabilities. Assume we want to run different checks on an applicant—credit, criminal records,

---

1. See the Decorator pattern in Gamma et al.'s *Design Patterns: Elements of Reusable Object-Oriented Software* [GHJV95].

employment, and so on. We're not interested in all the checks all the time. An applicant for an apartment may need to be checked for credit and criminal records. On the other hand, an applicant for employment may need to be checked for criminal records and previous employment. If we resort to creating specific classes for these groups of checks, we'll end up creating several classes for each permutation of checks we needed. Furthermore, if we decide to run additional checks, the class handling that group of checks would have to change. No, we want to avoid such class proliferation. We can be productive and mix in only specific checks required for each situation.

Next we'll introduce an abstract class Check that runs a general check on the application details:

TraitsAndTypeConversions/Decorator.scala

```scala
abstract class Check {
  def check() : String = "Checked Application Details..."
}
```

For different types of checks like credit, criminal record, and employment, we create traits like these:

TraitsAndTypeConversions/Decorator.scala

```scala
trait CreditCheck extends Check {
  override def check() : String = "Checked Credit..." + super.check()
}

trait EmploymentCheck extends Check {
  override def check() : String = "Checked Employment..." + super.check()
}

trait CriminalRecordCheck extends Check {
  override def check() : String = "Check Criminal Records..." + super.check()
}
```

We've extended these traits from the class Check since we intend to mix them into only those classes that extend from Check. Extending the class gives us two capabilities. One, these traits can be mixed in only with classes that extend Check. Second, we can use the methods of Check within these traits.

We are interested in enhancing or decorating the implementation of the method check(), so we have to mark it as override. In our implementation of check(), we invoke super.check(). Within a trait, calls to method using super go through late binding. This is not a call on the base class but instead on the trait mixed in to the left—if this is the leftmost trait mixed in, the call resolves to the method on the class into which we mixed in the trait(s). We'll see this behavior when we complete this example.

So, we have one abstract class and three traits in the example so far. We don't have any concrete classes—we don't need any. If we want to run checks for an apartment application, we can put together an instance from the previous traits and class:

TraitsAndTypeConversions/Decorator.scala

```scala
val apartmentApplication = new Check with CreditCheck with CriminalRecordCheck

println(apartmentApplication check)
```

On the other hand, we could run checks for employment like this:

TraitsAndTypeConversions/Decorator.scala

```scala
val emplomentApplication = new Check with CriminalRecordCheck with EmploymentCheck

println(emplomentApplication check)
```

If you'd rather run a different combination of checks, simply mix in the traits the way you like. The effect of previous two pieces of code is shown here:

```
Check Criminal Records...Checked Credit...Checked Application Details...
Checked Employment...Check Criminal Records...Checked Application Details...
```

The rightmost trait picked up the call to check(). It then, upon the call to super.check(), passed the call over to the trait on its left. The leftmost traits invoked the check() on the actual instance.

Traits are a powerful tool in Scala that allow you to mix in crosscutting concerns, and you can use them to create highly extensible code with low ceremony. Rather than creating a hierarchy of classes and interfaces, you can put your essential code to quick use.

7.4 Method Late Binding in Traits

In the previous example, the method check() of the Check class was concrete. Our traits extended from this class. We saw how the call to super.check() within the traits were bound to either the trait on the left or the class that mixes in. Things get a bit more complicated if the method(s) in the base class are abstract. Let's explore this further here.

Let us now write an abstract class Writer with one abstract method, writeMessage():

TraitsAndTypeConversions/MethodBinding.scala

```scala
abstract class Writer  {
  def writeMessage(message: String)
}
```

Any class extending from this class is required to implement the writeMessage() method. If we extend a trait from this abstract class and call the abstract method using super, Scala will demand that we declare the method as abstract override. The combination of these two keywords may seem odd to you. By using the keyword override, we are telling Scala that we are providing an implementation of a known method from the base class. At the same time, we are saying that the actual final "terminal" implementation for this method will be provided by the class that mixes in the trait. So, here is an example of traits that extend the previous class:

TraitsAndTypeConversions/MethodBinding.scala

```scala
trait UpperCaseWriter extends Writer {
  abstract override def writeMessage(message: String) =
    super.writeMessage(message.toUpperCase)
}

trait ProfanityFilteredWriter extends Writer {
  abstract override def writeMessage(message: String) =
    super.writeMessage(message.replace("stupid", "s-----"))
}
```

Scala does two things on the call to super.writeMessage in this code. First, it performs late binding of that call. Second, it will insist that the class that mixes these traits provide an implementation of the method. The ProfanityFilteredWriter took care of a mild rude word only—and only if it appeared in lowercase. This is with the intent to illustrate the ordering of the mixin.

Now, let's make use of these traits. First, let's write a class StringWriterDelegate that extends from the abstract class Writer and delegates writing the message to an instance of StringWriter:

TraitsAndTypeConversions/MethodBinding.scala

```scala
class StringWriterDelegate extends Writer {
  val writer = new java.io.StringWriter

  def writeMessage(message: String) = writer.write(message)
  override def toString() : String = writer.toString
}
```

We could have mixed in one or more traits in the previous definition of StringWriterDelegate. Instead, let's mix in the traits at the time of creating an instance of this class.

TraitsAndTypeConversions/MethodBinding.scala

```
val myWriterProfanityFirst =
  new StringWriterDelegate with UpperCaseWriter with ProfanityFilteredWriter

val myWriterProfanityLast =
  new StringWriterDelegate with ProfanityFilteredWriter with UpperCaseWriter

myWriterProfanityFirst writeMessage "There is no sin except stupidity"
myWriterProfanityLast writeMessage "There is no sin except stupidity"

println(myWriterProfanityFirst)
println(myWriterProfanityLast)
```

Since the ProfanityFilteredWriter is the rightmost trait in the first statement, it takes effect first. However, it takes effect second in the example in the second statement. Take the time to study the code. The method execution sequence for the two instances is shown here:

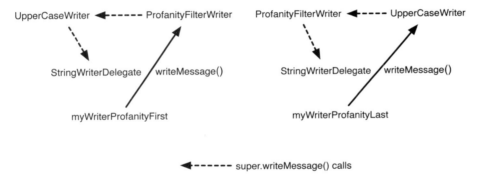

Here's our output:

```
THERE IS NO SIN EXCEPT S-----ITY
THERE IS NO SIN EXCEPT STUPIDITY
```

7.5 Implicit Type Conversions

Assume we're creating an application that involves several date and time operations. It'd be quite convenient and more readable to write code like the following:

```
2 days ago
5 days from_now
```

The previous looks more like data input rather than code—one of the characteristics of DSLs. An optional dot and parentheses help here. We are calling a method days() on 2 and sending in a variable ago in the first statement. In the second statement, we are calling the method on 5 and sending in a variable from_now.

If we try to compile the previous code, Scala will complain that days() is not a method on Int. Yes, Int does not provide us with that method, but that should not stop us from writing such code. We can ask Scala to quietly convert the Int to something that will help us accomplish the previous operation—enter implicit type conversion.

Implicit type conversion can help you extend the language to create your own vocabulary or syntax that's specific to your application and its domain or to create your own domain-specific languages.

Let's start with some crufty code to first understand the concept and then refactor that into a nice class.

We need to define the variables ago and from_now and ask Scala to accept the days() method. Defining variables is simple, but for it to accept the method, let's create a class DateHelper that takes an Int as a constructor parameter:

```
import java.util._

class DateHelper(number: Int) {
  def days(when: String) : Date = {
    var date = Calendar.getInstance()
    when match {
      case "ago" => date.add(Calendar.DAY_OF_MONTH, -number)
      case "from_now" => date.add(Calendar.DAY_OF_MONTH, number)
      case _ => date
    }
    date.getTime()
  }
}
```

The DateHelper class provides the days() method we want.[2] Now, all we have to do is convert an Int to a DateHelper. We can do this using a method that accepts an Int and returns an instance of DateHelper. Simply mark the method as implicit, and Scala will automatically pick it up if it is present in the current scope (visible through current imports or present in the current file).

---

2. The match() method used in the days() method is part of Scala's pattern matching facility discussed in Chapter 9, *Pattern Matching and Regular Expressions*, on page 109.

Here's the code for that:

```
implicit def convertInt2DateHelper(number: Int) = new DateHelper(number)

val ago = "ago"
val from_now = "from_now"

val past = 2 days ago
val appointment = 5 days from_now

println(past)
println(appointment)
```

If you run the previous code along with the definition of DateHelper, you'll see that Scala automatically converts the given numbers into an instance of DateHelper and invokes the days() method.

Now that the code works, it's time to clean it up a bit. We don't want to write the implicit converter each time we need the conversion. By tucking away the converter into a separate singleton object, we get better reusability and ease of use. Let's move the converter to the companion object of DateHelper:

TraitsAndTypeConversions/DateHelper.scala
```
import java.util._

class DateHelper(number: Int) {
  def days(when: String) : Date = {
    var date = Calendar.getInstance()
    when match {
      case DateHelper.ago => date.add(Calendar.DAY_OF_MONTH, -number)
      case DateHelper.from_now => date.add(Calendar.DAY_OF_MONTH, number)
      case _ => date
    }
    date.getTime()
  }
}

object DateHelper {
  val ago = "ago"
  val from_now = "from_now"

  implicit def convertInt2DateHelper(number: Int) = new DateHelper(number)
}
```

When we import DateHelper, Scala will automatically find the converter for us. This is because Scala applies conversions in the current scope and in the scope of what we import.

Here's an example of using the implicit conversion we wrote in the Date-Helper:

TraitsAndTypeConversions/DaysDSL.scala

```
import DateHelper._

val past = 2 days ago
val appointment = 5 days from_now

println(past)
println(appointment)
```

Here's the result:

```
Sun Dec 07 13:11:06 MST 2008
Sun Dec 14 13:11:06 MST 2008
```

Scala has a number of implicit conversions already defined in the Predef object, which is imported by default. So, for example, when we write 1 to 3, Scala implicitly converts 1 from Int to the rich wrapper RichInt and invokes its to() method.

Scala applies at most one implicit conversion at a time. The conversion, in the current scope, is applied when it finds that by converting a type it can help an operation, method call, or type conversion succeed.

In this chapter, you learned about two interesting scala features, traits and implicit conversion. These two concepts can help you create extensible code with dynamic behavior beyond what's provided by one single class. In the next chapter, you'll take a look at Scala's support for collections of objects.

Chapter 8
Using Collections

In this chapter, you'll learn how to create instances of common Scala collections and how to iterate through them. You can still use the collections from the JDK such as ArrayList, Vector, and simple arrays, but in this chapter you'll focus on the Scala-specific collections List, Set, and Map and how to work with them.

8.1 Common Scala Collections

Scala's main collections are List, Set, and Map. As you would expect, a list is an ordered collection of objects, a set is an unordered collection, and a map is a dictionary of key-value pairs. Scala favors immutable collections, even though mutable versions are also provided. If you want to modify a collection and your operations on the collection are all within a single thread, you can choose a mutable collection. However, if you plan to use the collection across threads or actors, the immutable collections are better. Immutable collections are not only thread safe, but they are free from side effects and help with program correctness. You can choose between these versions by selecting a class in one of these two packages: scala.collection.mutable or scala.collection.immutable.

UsingCollections/UsingSet.scala

```scala
val colors1 = Set("Blue", "Green", "Red")
var colors = colors1
println("colors1 (colors): " + colors)

colors += "Black"
println("colors: " + colors)
println("colors1: " + colors1)
```

In the previous example, we started with a Set of three colors. When we added the color black, we did not modify the original set. We got a new set with four elements, as shown here:

```
colors1 (colors): Set(Blue, Green, Red)
colors: Set(Blue, Green, Red, Black)
colors1: Set(Blue, Green, Red)
```

By default we used the immutable set. This is because the default included object Predef provides aliases for Set and Map to point to the immutable implementations. Set and Map are traits in the Scala package scala.collection that are refined by corresponding mutable versions in the package scala.collection.mutable and by immutable versions in scala.collection.immutable.

In the previous example, we created an instance of Set without using a new. So, instead of writing the following:

```
val colors1 = new scala.collection.immutable.Set3[String]("Blue", "Green", "Red")
```

we can use a concise val colors1 = Set("Blue", "Green", "Red").[1] It was able to figure out that we need a Set[String]. Similarly, if we write Set(1, 2, 3), we'll get a Set[Int]. This magic is possible because of a special apply() method, also called a *factory method*. A statement like X(...), where X is a class name or an instance reference, is treated as X.apply(...). So, Scala automatically calls an apply() method on the companion object of the class, if present. The apply() method is available on Map and List as well.

8.2 Using a Set

Suppose we're writing an RSS feed reader and we want to frequently update the feeds, but we don't care about the order. We can store the feed URLs in a Set. Assume we have the following feeds stored in two Sets:

```
val feeds1 = Set("blog.toolshed.com", "pragdave.pragprog.com",
  "pragmactic-osxer.blogspot.com", "vita-contemplativa.blogspot.com")
val feeds2 = Set("blog.toolshed.com", "martinfowler.com/bliki")
```

If we want to update only select feeds from feeds1, say the ones that are on Blogspot, we can get those feeds using the filter() methods:

```
val blogSpotFeeds = feeds1 filter ( _ contains "blogspot" )
println("blogspot feeds: " + blogSpotFeeds.mkString(", "))
```

---

1. Set3 is a class that represents an implementation of a set with three elements.

We'll get this output:

```
blogspot feeds: pragmactic-osxer.blogspot.com, vita-contemplativa.blogspot.com
```

The mkString() method helps create a string representation of each element of a Set and concatenates the results with the argument string (a comma in this example).

If we need to merge two Sets of feeds to create a new Set, we can use the ++():

```
val mergedFeeds = feeds1 ++ feeds2
println("# of merged feeds: " + mergedFeeds.size)
```

Set will hold an element at most once, so, as you can see in the output, the common feeds in the two sets will be stored only once in the merged set:

```
# of merged feeds: 5
```

If we need to compare notes and find what common feeds we have with a friend's, we can import our friend's feeds and perform the intersect operation (**()):

```
val commonFeeds = feeds1 ** feeds2
println("common feeds: " + commonFeeds.mkString(", "))
```

Here's the effect of the intersect operation on the two previous feeds:

```
common feeds: blog.toolshed.com
```

If we want to prefix each feed with the string "http://," we can use the map() method. This method applies the given function value to each element, collects the result into a Set, and finally returns the resulting set. If we'd like to access the elements of a Set using an index, we can copy the elements into an array using the toArray() method:

```
val urls = feeds1 map ( "http://" + _ )
println("One url: " + urls.toArray(0))
```

We should see this:

```
One url: http://blog.toolshed.com
```

Finally, when we're ready to iterate over the feeds and refresh them one at a time, we can use the built-in iterator foreach() like this:

```
println("Refresh Feeds:")
feeds1 foreach { feed => println("  Refreshing " + feed ) }
```

Here's the result:

```
Refresh Feeds:
  Refreshing blog.toolshed.com
```

```
Refreshing pragdave.pragprog.com
Refreshing pragmactic-osxer.blogspot.com
Refreshing vita-contemplativa.blogspot.com
```

8.3 Using a Map

We just used a Set to store feeds. Suppose we want to attach the feed author's name to feeds; we can store it as a key-value pair in a Map:

```
val feeds = Map("Andy Hunt" -> "blog.toolshed.com",
  "Dave Thomas" -> "pragdave.pragprog.com",
  "Dan Steinberg" -> "dimsumthinking.com/blog")
```

If we want to get a Map of feeds for folks whose name starts with "D," we can use the filterKeys() method:

```
val filterNameStartWithD = feeds filterKeys( _ startsWith "D" )
println("# of Filtered: " + filterNameStartWithD.size)
```

Here's the result:

```
# of Filtered: 2
```

On the other hand, if we want to filter on the values, in addition to or instead of the keys, we can use the filter() method. The function value we provide to filter() receives a (key, value) tuple, and we can use it as in this example:

```
val filterNameStartWithDAndBlogInFeed = feeds filter { element =>
  val (key, value) = element
  (key startsWith "D") && (value contains "blog")
}
println("# of feeds with auth name D* and blog in URL: " +
  filterNameStartWithDAndBlogInFeed.size)
```

Here's our output:

```
# of feeds with auth name D* and blog in URL: 1
```

If we want to get a feed for a person, simply use the get() method. Since there may not be a value for the given key, the return type of get() is Option[T], and the result may be either a Some[T] or a None, where T is the type of values in the Map:

```
println("Get Andy's Feed: " + feeds.get("Andy Hunt"))
println("Get Bill's Feed: " + feeds.get("Bill Who"))
```

The output from the previous code is shown here:

```
Get Andy's Feed: Some(blog.toolshed.com)
Get Bill's Feed: None
```

Alternately, we can use the apply() method to get the values for a key—remember, this is the method Scala calls when we use parentheses on a class or an instance. The apply() method, however, instead of returning Option[T], returns the value. Unlike get(), if there's no value for a given key, it throws an exception. So, make sure to place the code within a try-catch block:

```
try {
  println("Get Andy's Feed Using apply(): " + feeds("Andy Hunt"))
  print("Get Bill's Feed: ")
  println(feeds("Bill Who"))
}
catch {
  case ex : java.util.NoSuchElementException => println("Not found")
}
```

Here's the output from the use of apply():

```
Get Andy's Feed Using apply(): blog.toolshed.com
Get Bill's Feed: Not found
```

If we'd like to add a feed, use the update() method. Since we're working with an immutable collection, the update() does not affect the original Map. Instead, it returns a new Map with the added element:

```
val newFeeds1 = feeds.update("Venkat Subramaniam", "agiledeveloper.com/blog")
println("Venkat's blog in original feeds: " + feeds.get("Venkat Subramaniam"))
println("Venkat's blog in new feed: " + newFeeds1("Venkat Subramaniam"))
```

We can see the effect of update():

```
Venkat's blog in original feeds: None
Venkat's blog in new feed: agiledeveloper.com/blog
```

Instead of calling update() explicitly, you can take advantage of another Scala trick. If you use the parentheses on a class or instance on the left side of an assignment, Scala automatically calls the update() method. So, X() = b is equivalent to X.update(b). If update() takes more than one parameter, you can place all but the trailing parameter within the parentheses. So, X(a) = b is equivalent to X.update(a, b).

We can use the implicit call on immutable collections, like this: val newFeed = feeds("author") = "blog". However, it loses the syntactic elegance because of multiple assignments, one for the update() and the other to save the newly created Map. If we were returning the newly created map from a method, the implicit update() is elegant to use. However, if our intent is to update the map in place, it makes more sense to use the implicit call on mutable collections.

```
val mutableFeeds = scala.collection.mutable.Map(
    "Scala Book Forum" -> "forums.pragprog.com/forums/87")
mutableFeeds("Groovy Book Forum") = "forums.pragprog.com/forums/55"
println("Number of forums: " + mutableFeeds.size)
```

We get the following result:

```
Number of forums: 2
```

8.4 Using a List

Unlike Set and Map, which have mutable and immutable implementations, List comes only in the immutable flavor. Scala makes it easier and faster to access the first element of a list using the head method. Everything except the first element can be accessed using the tail method. Accessing the last element of the list requires traversing the list and so is more expensive than accessing the head and the tail. So, most operations on the list are structured around operations on the head and tail.

Let's continue with the feeds example. We can maintain an ordered collection of the feeds using a List:

```
val feeds = List("blog.toolshed.com", "pragdave.pragprog.com",
    "dimsumthinking.com/blog")
```

This creates an instance of List[String]. We can access the elements of the List using an index from 0 to list.length - 1.[2] To access the first element, we can use either feeds(0) or the head() method:

```
println("First feed: " + feeds.head)
println("Second feed: " + feeds(1))
```

The output from the previous code is shown here:

```
First feed: blog.toolshed.com
Second feed: pragdave.pragprog.com
```

If we want to prefix an element, that is, place it in the front of the list, we can use the special method ::(). Read a :: list as "prefix a to the list." This method is an operation on the list, even though the list follows the operator; see Section 8.4, *Method Name Convention*, on page 103 for details on how this works.

```
val prefixedList = "forums.pragprog.com/forums/87" :: feeds
println("First Feed In Prefixed: " + prefixedList.head)
```

---

2. When we invoke feeds(1), we're using List's apply() method.

The output from the previous code is shown here:

```
First Feed In Prefixed: forums.pragprog.com/forums/87
```

Suppose we want to append a list, say listA, to another, say list. We would achieve that by actually prefixing list to the listA using the :::() method. So, the code would be list ::: listA and would read "prefix list to listA." Since lists are immutable, we did not affect either one of the previous lists. We simply created a new one with elements from both. Here's an example of appending:

```
val feedsWithForums =
  feeds ::: List("forums.pragprog.com/forums/87", "forums.pragprog.com/forums/55")
println("First feed in feeds with forum: " + feedsWithForums.head)
println("Last feed in feeds with forum: " + feedsWithForums.last)
```

And here's the output:

```
First feed in feeds with forum: blog.toolshed.com
Last feed in feeds with forum: forums.pragprog.com/forums/55
```

Again, the method :::() is called on the list that follows the operator.

To append an element to our list, we can use the same :::() method. First we place the element we'd like to append into a list and prefix the original list to it:

```
val appendedList = feeds ::: List("agiledeveloper.com/blog")
println("Last Feed In Appended: " + appendedList.last)
```

We should see this output:

```
Last Feed In Appended: agiledeveloper.com/blog
```

Notice that to append an element or a list to another list, we actually used the prefix operator on the latter. The reason for this is that it's much faster to access the head element of a list than to traverse to its last element. So, the same result is achieved but with better performance.

To select only feeds that satisfy some condition, use the filter() method. If we want to check whether all feeds meet a certain condition, we can use the forall(). If, on the other hand, we want to know whether any feed meets a certain condition, exists() will help us.

```
println("Feeds with blog: " + feeds.filter( _ contains "blog" ).mkString(", "))
println("All feeds have com: " + feeds.forall( _ contains "com" ))
println("All feeds have dave: " + feeds.forall( _ contains "dave" ))
println("Any feed has dave: " + feeds.exists( _ contains "dave" ))
println("Any feed has bill: " + feeds.exists( _ contains "bill" ))
```

We'll get this:

```
Feeds with blog: blog.toolshed.com, dimsumthinking.com/blog
All feeds have com: true
All feeds have dave: false
Any feed has dave: true
Any feed has bill: false
```

Suppose we need to know the number of characters we need to display each feed name. We can use the map() method to work on each element to get a list of the result, as shown here:

```
println("Feed url lengths: " + feeds.map( _.length ).mkString(", "))
```

Here's our output:

```
Feed url lengths: 17, 21, 23
```

If we're interested in the total number of characters of all feeds put together, we can use the foldLeft() method like this:

```
val total = feeds.foldLeft(0) { (total, feed) => total + feed.length }
println("Total length of feed urls: " + total )
```

The output from the previous code is shown here:

```
Total length of feed urls: 61
```

Notice that although the previous method is performing the summation, it did not deal with any mutable state. It is pure functional style. A new updated value was accumulated as the method progressed through the elements in the list without changing anything, however.

The foldLeft() method will invoke the given function value (code block) for each element in the list, starting from the left. It passes two parameters to the function value. The first parameter is a partial result from the execution of the function value for the previous element (which is why it's called *folding*—it's as if the list is folded into the result of these computations). The second parameter is an element in the list. The initial value for the partial result is provided as the parameter to the method (Zero in this example). The foldLeft() method forms a chain of elements and carries the partial result of computation in the function value from one element to the next, starting from the left. Similarly, foldRight() will do the same, starting at the right.

Scala provides alternate methods to make the previous methods concise.[3] The method /:() is equivalent to foldLeft() and \:() to foldRight(). Here is the previous example written using /::

```scala
val total2 = (0 /: feeds) { (total, feed) => total + feed.length }
println("Total length of feed urls: " + total2 )
```

The output from the previous code is shown here:

```
Total length of feed urls: 61
```

We can reach out to Scala conventions here and make the code even more concise as follows:

```scala
val total3 = (0 /: feeds) { _ + _.length }
println("Total length of feed urls: " + total3 )
```

Here's our output:

```
Total length of feed urls: 61
```

I have shown here some interesting methods of List. There are several other methods in List that provide additional capabilities. For a complete documentation, refer to "The Scala Language API" in Appendix A, on page 207.

Method Name Convention

In Section 3.6, *Operator Overloading*, on page 34, you saw how Scala supports operator overloading even though it does not have operators. Operators are methods with crafty method naming convention. You saw that the first character of a method decides the precedence (see Section 3.6, *Operator Overloading*, on page 34). Here you see that the last character of their names also has an effect—it determines the target of the method call.

The convention of : may surprise you at first, but as you get used to it (or as you "develop a Scala eye" as I like to put it), you'll see it improves fluency. For example, if we want to prefix a value to a list, we can write it as value :: list. Although it reads "value is prefixed to the list," the target of the method is actually the list with the value as the argument, that is, list.::(value).

---

3. You will either love this conciseness, like I do, or hate it. I don't think there will be anything in between.

If a method name ends with a colon (:), then the target of the call is the instance that follows the operator.[4] In this next example, ∧() is a method defined on the class Cow, while ∧:() is a method defined on the class Moon:

`Scalaldioms/Colon.scala`

```scala
class Cow {
  def ∧(moon: Moon) = println("Cow jumped over the moon")
}

class Moon {
  def ∧:(cow: Cow) = println("This cow jumped over the moon too")
}
```

Here is an example of using these two methods:

`Scalaldioms/Colon.scala`

```scala
val cow = new Cow
val moon = new Moon

cow ∧ moon
cow ∧: moon
```

In the previous code, our calls to the two methods look almost identical, the cow to the left and the moon to the right of the operators. However, the first call is on cow, while the second call is on moon; the difference is so subtle. It can be quite frustrating for someone new to Scala, but this convention is quite common in list operations, so you'd better get used to it. The output from the previous code looks like this:

```
Cow jumped over the moon
This cow jumped over the moon too
```

The last call in the previous example is equivalent to this code as well:

```scala
moon.∧:(cow)
```

In addition to operators that end with :, there are a set of operators that also are targeted at the instance that follow them. These are the unary operators +, -, !, and ~. The unary + maps over to a call to unary_+(), the unary - to unary_-(), and so on.

---

4. Scala does not permit an operator to succeed a method name with alphanumeric characters, unless we prefix that operator with an underscore. So, a method named jumpOver:() is rejected, but jumpOver_:() is accepted.

Here's an example of defining unary operators on a Sample class:

Scalaidioms/Unary.scala

```scala
class Sample {
  def unary_+ = println("Called unary +")
  def unary_- = println("called unary -")
  def unary_! = println("called unary !")
  def unary_~ = println("called unary ~")
}

val sample = new Sample
+sample
-sample
!sample
~sample
```

The output from the previous code is shown here:

```
Called unary +
called unary -
called unary !
called unary ~
```

As you get comfortable with Scala, you'll develop a Scala eye—soon the mental processing of these notations and conventions will become subliminal.

8.5 The for Expression

The foreach() method provides internal iterators on collections—you don't control the looping. You simply provide code to execute in the context of each iteration. However, if you'd like to control the looping or work with multiple collections at the same time, you can use an external iterator, the for() expression. Let's look at a simple loop:

Scalaidioms/PowerOfFor.scala

```scala
for (i <- 1 to 3) { print("ho ") }
```

The previous code prints "ho ho ho." It's a short form of the general syntax of the following expression:

```scala
for([pattern <- generator; definition*]+; filter*)
  [yield] expression
```

The for expression takes as a parameter one or more generators, with zero or more definitions and zero or more filters. These are separated from each other by semicolons. The yield keyword is optional and, if present, tells the expression to return a list of values instead of a Unit. That was a boatload of details, but don't worry, because we'll take a look at it with examples, so you will get quite comfortable with it in no time.

Let's start with the yield first. Suppose we want to take values in a range and multiply each value by 2. Here's a code example to do that:

Scalaldioms/PowerOfFor.scala
```
val result = for (i <- 1 to 10)
  yield i * 2
```

The previous code returns a collection of values where each value is a double of the values in the given range 1 to 10.

We could've also performed the previous logic using the map() method like this:

Scalaldioms/PowerOfFor.scala
```
val result2 = (1 to 10).map(_ * 2)
```

Behind the scenes, Scala translates the for expression into an expression that uses a combination of methods like map() and filter() depending on the complexity of the expression.

Now suppose we want to double only even numbers in the range. We can use a filter:

Scalaldioms/PowerOfFor.scala
```
val doubleEven = for (i <- 1 to 10; if i % 2 == 0)
    yield i * 2
```

Read the previous for expression as "Return a collection of i * 2 where i is a member of the given range and i is even." So, the previous expression is really like a SQL query on a collection of values—this is called *list comprehension* in functional programming.

If you find the semicolons in the previous code too noisy, you can drop them by using curly braces instead of parentheses like this:

```
for {
  i <- 1 to 10
  if i % 2 == 0
}
 yield i * 2
```

We can place a definition along with a generator. Scala defines a new val with that name through each iteration.

Here is an example of iterating over a collection of Person and printing their last names:

```
Scalaldioms/Friends.scala
```

```scala
class Person(val firstName: String, val lastName: String)
object Person {
  def apply(firstName: String, lastName: String) : Person =
    new Person(firstName, lastName)
}

val friends = List(Person("Brian", "Sletten"), Person("Neal", "Ford"),
  Person("Scott", "Davis"), Person("Stuart", "Halloway"))

val lastNames = for (friend <- friends; lastName = friend.lastName) yield lastName

println(lastNames.mkString(", "))
```

The output from the previous code is shown here:

```
Sletten, Ford, Davis, Halloway
```

The previous code is also an example of the Scala syntax sugar where the apply() method is working under the covers—the code is concise and readable, but we've created a new list of Persons.

If you provide more than one generator in the for expression, each generator forms an inner loop, with the rightmost generator controlling the innermost loop. Here is an example of using two generators:

```
Scalaldioms/MultipleLoop.scala
```

```scala
for (i <- 1 to 3; j <- 4 to 6) {
  print("[" + i + "," + j + "] ")
}
```

The output from the previous code is shown here:

```
[1,4] [1,5] [1,6] [2,4] [2,5] [2,6] [3,4] [3,5] [3,6]
```

In this chapter, you learned how to use the three major collections provided in Scala. You also saw the power of the for() expression and list comprehension. Next you'll learn about pattern matching, one of the most powerful features in Scala.

Chapter 9

Pattern Matching and Regular Expressions

Pattern matching is the second most widely used feature of Scala, after function values and closures. You will use it quite extensively when you receive messages from actors in concurrent programming. Scala has superb support for pattern matching for processing the messages you receive in different formats and types. In this chapter, you'll learn about Scala's mechanism for pattern matching, the case classes, and the extractors, as well as how to create and use regular expressions.

9.1 Matching Literals and Constants

You'll usually pass messages between actors as a String literal, a number, or a tuple. If your message is a literal, you don't have to do much to match it. Simply type the literal you'd like to match, and you're done. Suppose we need to determine activities for different days of the week. Assume we get the day as a String and we respond with our activity for that day. Here is an example of how we can pattern match the days:

PatternMatching/MatchLiterals.scala

```scala
def activity(day: String) {
  day match {
    case "Sunday" => print("Eat, sleep, repeat... ")
    case "Saturday" => print("Hangout with friends... ")
    case "Monday" => print("...code for fun...")
    case "Friday" => print("...read a good book...")
  }
}

List("Monday", "Sunday", "Saturday").foreach { activity }
```

The match is an expression that acts on Any. In this example, we're using it on a String. It performs pattern matching on the target and invokes the appropriate case expression with the matching pattern value. The output from the previous code is shown here:

```
...code for fun...Eat, sleep, repeat... Hangout with friends...
```

You can directly match against literals and constants. The literals can be different types; the match does not care. However, the type of the target object to the left of match may restrict the type. In the previous example, since this was of type String, the match could be any string.

The case expression is not limited to use within the match statement. Here, the block of code containing the case expression(s) is simply a function value.

9.2 Matching a Wildcard

In the previous example, we did not handle all possible values of day. If there is a value that is not matched by one of the case expressions, we'll get a MatchError exception. We can control the values day can take by making the parameter an enum instead of a String. Even then we may not want to handle each day of the week. We can avoid the exception by using a wildcard:

PatternMatching/Wildcard.scala

```scala
object DayOfWeek extends Enumeration {
  val SUNDAY = Value("Sunday")
  val MONDAY = Value("Monday")
  val TUESDAY = Value("Tuesday")
  val WEDNESDAY = Value("Wednesday")
  val THURSDAY = Value("Thursday")
  val FRIDAY = Value("Friday")
  val SATURDAY = Value("Saturday")
}

def activity(day: DayOfWeek.Value) {
  day match {
    case DayOfWeek.SUNDAY => println("Eat, sleep, repeat...")
    case DayOfWeek.SATURDAY => println("Hangout with friends")
    case _ => println("...code for fun...")
  }
}

activity(DayOfWeek.SATURDAY)
activity(DayOfWeek.MONDAY)
```

In the previous code, we've defined an enumeration for the days of the week. We can use Java enums in Scala. However, if we want to create them in Scala, extend a singleton object from scala.Enumeration as shown. In our activity() method, we matched SUNDAY and SATURDAY and let the wildcard, represented by an underscore (_), handle the rest of the days.

If we run the code, we'll get this match of SATURDAY followed by MONDAY being matched by the wildcard:

```
Hangout with friends
...code for fun...
```

9.3 Matching Tuples and Lists

Matching literals and enumerations is simple. But, soon you'll realize your messages are not single literals but a sequence of values in the form of either tuples or lists. You can use the case expression to match against tuples and lists. Suppose we are writing a service that needs to receive and process geographic coordinates. The coordinates can be represented as a tuple that we can match like this:

PatternMatching/MatchTuples.scala

```
def processCoordinates(input: Any) {
  input match {
    case (a, b) => printf("Processing (%d, %d)... ", a, b)
    case "done" => println("done")
    case _ => null
  }
}

processCoordinates((39, -104))
processCoordinates("done")
```

This matches any tuple with two values in it, plus the literal "done." We'll get something like this:

```
Processing (39, -104)... done
```

If the argument we send is not a tuple with two elements or does not match "done," then the wildcard will handle it. The printf() statement has a hidden assumption that the values in the tuple are integers. If they're not, our code will fail at runtime—that's not good. We can avoid that by providing type information for matches, as you'll see in Section 9.4, *Matching with Types and Guards*, on the next page.

You can match Lists the same way you matched tuples. Simply provide the elements you care about, and you can leave out the rest using the array explosion symbol (_*):

`PatternMatching/MatchList.scala`

```scala
def processItems(items: List[String]) {
  items match {
    case List("apple", "ibm") => println("Apples and IBMs")
    case List("red", "blue", "white") => println("Stars and Stripes...")
    case List("red", "blue", _*) => println("colors red, blue, ... ")
    case List("apple", "orange", otherFruits @ _*) =>
      println("apples, oranges, and " + otherFruits)
  }
}

processItems(List("apple", "ibm"))
processItems(List("red", "blue", "green"))
processItems(List("red", "blue", "white"))
processItems(List("apple", "orange", "grapes", "dates"))
```

In the first and second case, we expected two and three specific items in the List, respectively. In the remaining two cases, we expect two or more items, but the first two items must be as specified. If we need to reference the remaining matching elements, we can place a variable name (like otherFruits) before a special @ symbol as in the previous code. The output from the previous code is shown here:

```
Apples and IBMs
colors red, blue, ...
Stars and Stripes...
apples, oranges, and List(grapes, dates)
```

9.4 Matching with Types and Guards

You will often want to handle a sequence of values that are not all of the same type. You may want to handle a sequence of, say, Ints differently from how you handle a sequence of Doubles. Scala lets you ask the case statement to match against types.

`PatternMatching/MatchTypes.scala`

```scala
Line 1  def process(input: Any) {
   -      input match {
   -        case (a: Int, b: Int) => print("Processing (int, int)... ")
   -        case (a: Double, b: Double) => print("Processing (double, double)... ")
   5        case msg : Int if (msg > 1000000) => println("Processing int > 1000000")
   -        case msg : Int => print("Processing int... ")
   -        case msg: String => println("Processing string... ")
   -        case _ => printf("Can't handle %s... ", input)
   -      }
   10 }
```

```
 -   process((34.2, -159.3))
 -   process(0)
 -   process(1000001)
15   process(2.2)
```

You can see how to specify types for single values and elements of a tuple in the case. In addition to types, you can also use guards. In addition to matching the pattern, the guard provided using the if clause must also be satisfied for the expression to evaluate.

The order of the case is important. Scala will evaluate from the top down. So, for example, we can't swap line numbers 5 and 6 in the previous code. The output from the previous code is shown here:

```
Processing (double, double)... Processing int... Processing int > 1000000
Can't handle 2.2...
```

9.5 Pattern Variables and Constants in case Expressions

You already saw how to define placeholder vals for what you're matching (like a and b when matching tuples). These are pattern variables. However, you have to use caution when defining them. By convention, Scala expects the pattern variables to start with a lowercase letter and expects constants to start with an uppercase letter. So, the following code will not compile. Scala will assume the max is a pattern variable even though we have a field with that name in the current scope. Scala, however, will match the MIN without trouble because it starts with an uppercase letter.

PatternMatching/MatchWithValsError.scala

```
class Sample {
  val max = 100
  val MIN = 0

  def process(input: Int) {
    input match {
      case max => println("Don't try this at home") // Compiler error
      case MIN => println("You matched min")
      case _ => println("Unreachable!!")
    }
  }
}
```

You can refer to the offending fields in the case expression with explicit scoping (like ObjectName.fieldName if ObjectName is a singleton or companion object or obj.fieldName if obj is a reference).

The previous code can be fixed like this:

PatternMatching/MatchWithValsOK.scala

```scala
class Sample {
  val max = 100
  val MIN = 0

  def process(input: Int) {
    input match {
      case this.max => println("You matched max")
      case MIN => println("You matched min")
      case _ => println("Unmatched")
    }
  }
}

new Sample().process(100)
new Sample().process(0)
new Sample().process(10)
```

Now we'll get this output:

```
You matched max
You matched min
Unmatched
```

In a realistic application, you will soon outgrow matching simple literals, lists, tuples, and objects. You'll want to match against more complicated patterns. Two options are available for you in Scala: case classes and *extractors*. Let's take a look at each of these in turn.

9.6 Pattern Matching XML Fragments

Scala allows you to easily pattern match XML fragments. You don't have to embed XML into strings. You can directly place the XML fragments as parameters to the case statement. The capability is quite powerful; however, because we need to first discuss XML handling in Scala, I'll defer this topic to Chapter 14, *Using Scala*, on page 183.

9.7 Matching Using case Classes

case classes are special classes that are used in pattern matching with case expressions. Suppose we want to receive and process stock-trading transactions. The messages for selling and buying might be accompanied with information such as the name of a stock and a quantity. It is convenient to store this information in objects, but how would we pattern match them? This is the purpose of case classes. These are classes that the pattern matcher readily recognizes and matches. Here is an example of a few case classes:

PatternMatching/TradeProcessor.scala

```
abstract case class Trade()
case class Sell(stockSymbol: String, quantity: Int) extends Trade
case class Buy(stockSymbol: String, quantity: Int) extends Trade
case class Hedge(stockSymbol: String, quantity: Int) extends Trade
```

We've defined Trade as abstract since we don't expect instances of it. We have extended Sell, Buy, and Hedge from it. These three take a stock symbol and quantity as parameters.

Now we can use these in case statements, as shown here:

PatternMatching/TradeProcessor.scala

```
class TradeProcessor {
  def processTransaction(request : Trade) {
    request match {
      case Sell(stock, 1000) => println("Selling 1000-units of " + stock)
      case Sell(stock, quantity) =>
          printf("Selling %d units of %s\n", quantity, stock)
      case Buy(stock, quantity) if (quantity > 2000) =>
        printf("Buying %d (large) units of %s\n", quantity, stock)
      case Buy(stock, quantity) =>
          printf("Buying %d units of %s\n", quantity, stock)
    }
  }
}
```

We match the request against Sell and Buy. The stock symbol and quantity we receive are matched and stored in the pattern variables stock and quantity, respectively. We can specify constant values (like 1000 for quantity) or even use a guarded match (like checking if quantity > 2000). Here is an example of using the TradeProcessor class:

PatternMatching/TradeStock.scala

```
val tradeProcessor = new TradeProcessor
tradeProcessor.processTransaction(Sell("GOOG", 500))
tradeProcessor.processTransaction(Buy("GOOG", 700))
tradeProcessor.processTransaction(Sell("GOOG", 1000))
tradeProcessor.processTransaction(Buy("GOOG", 3000))
```

The output from the previous code is shown here:

```
Selling 500 units of GOOG
Buying 700 units of GOOG
Selling 1000-units of GOOG
Buying 3000 (large) units of GOOG
```

In processTransaction(), we did not match all possible types of Trades; we skipped Hedge. This will be a problem at runtime if a Hedge is received. However, Scala does not know how many case classes inherit from Trade. After all, we may have extended other case classes in other files. Scala can, however, help if we tell Scala that we have no more classes than presented in this file. We can do this by using an unusual combination of sealed abstract, as shown here:

```
sealed abstract case class Trade()
case class Sell(stockSymbol: String, quantity: Int) extends Trade
case class Buy(stockSymbol: String, quantity: Int) extends Trade
case class Hedge(stockSymbol: String, quantity: Int) extends Trade
```

Now, if we compile the TradeProcessor class, the Scala compiler will yell out "warning: match is not exhaustive!" Add a case for Hedge to fix this warning. In the previous example, all the concrete case classes took parameters. If you have a case class that takes no parameter, remember to place parentheses when you use it (see "Hittin' the Edge Cases" in Appendix A, on page 207). In the following example, we have case classes that don't take any parameters:

PatternMatching/ThingsAcceptor.scala
```
import scala.actors._
import Actor._

case class Apple()
case class Orange()
case class Book ()

class ThingsAcceptor {
  def acceptStuff(thing: Any) {
    thing match {
      case Apple() => println("Thanks for the Apple")
      case Orange() => println("Thanks for the Orange")
      case Book() => println("Thanks for the Book")
      case _ => println("Excuse me, why did you send me a " + thing)
    }
  }
}
```

In the following code, we forgot to place parentheses next to Apple in one of the calls:

PatternMatching/UseThingsAcceptor.scala
```
val acceptor = new ThingsAcceptor
acceptor.acceptStuff(Apple())
acceptor.acceptStuff(Book())
acceptor.acceptStuff(Apple)
```

The result of the previous calls is shown here:

```
Thanks for the Apple
Thanks for the Book
Excuse me, why did you send me a <function>
```

When we forgot the parentheses, instead of sending an instance of the case class, we are sending its companion object. The companion object mixes in the scala.Function0 trait, meaning it can be treated as a function. So, we end up sending in a function instead of an instance of the case class. If the acceptStuff() method received an instance of a case class named Thing, this would not be a problem. However, when you pass messages between actors, you can't control what is sent to your actors in such a type-safe manner at compile time. So, use caution when passing case classes.

Although the Scala compiler may evolve to fix the previous problem, these kinds of edge cases can still arise. This emphasizes the need for good testing even in a statically typed language (see Chapter 12, *Unit Testing with Scala*, on page 163).

9.8 Matching Using Extractors

You can take pattern matching to the next level of matching arbitrary patterns using Scala extractors. As the name indicates, an extractor will extract matching parts from the input. Suppose we are writing a service that will process stock-related input. The first task on hand is for us to receive a stock symbol and return the price for that stock (we'll print out the result for illustrative purposes here). Here is an example of calls we can expect:

```
StockService process "GOOG"
StockService process "IBM"
StockService process "ERR"
```

The process() method needs to validate if the given symbol is valid and, if it is, return the price for it. Here is the code for that:

```
object StockService {
  def process(input : String) {
    input match {
      case Symbol() => println("Look up price for valid symbol " + input)
      case _ => println("Invalid input " + input)
    }
  }
}
```

The process() method performs pattern matching using the yet-to-be-defined extractor Symbol. If the extractor determines the symbol is valid, it returns true; otherwise, it returns false. If it returns true, the expression associated with the case is executed. Otherwise, the pattern match continues to the next case. Let's take a look at the extractor:

```scala
object Symbol {
  def unapply(symbol : String) : Boolean = symbol == "GOOG" || symbol == "IBM"
    // you'd look up database above... here only GOOG and IBM are recognized
}
```

The extractor has one method named unapply() that accepts the value we'd like to match. The match expression automatically sends the input as a parameter to the unapply() method when case Symbol() => ... is executed. When we execute the previous three pieces of code (remember to put the sample calls to the service toward the bottom of your file), we will get the following output:

```
Look up price for valid symbol GOOG
Look up price for valid symbol IBM
Invalid input ERR
```

The unapply() may strike you as an odd name for a method. You may expect a method like evaluate() for the extractor. The reason for this method name is that the extractor can take an optional apply() method. These two methods, apply() and unapply(), perform the opposite actions. The unapply() breaks down the object into pieces that match a pattern, while the apply() is intended to optionally put it back together.

Now that we are able to ask for a stock quote, the next task given to us, for our service, is to set the price of a stock. Assume that the message for this arrives in the format "SYMBOL:PRICE." We need to pattern match this format and take action. Here is the modified process() method to handle this additional task:

PatternMatching/Extractor.scala
```scala
object StockService {
  def process(input : String) {
    input match {
      case Symbol() => println("Look up price for valid symbol " + input)
      case ReceiveStockPrice(symbol, price) =>
        printf("Received price %f for symbol %s\n", price, symbol)
      case _ => println("Invalid input " + input)
    }
  }
}
```

We've added a new case with a yet-to-be-written extractor ReceiveStock-Price. This extractor will be different from the Symbol extractor we wrote earlier. The latter simply returned a boolean result. ReceiveStockPrice, however, needs to parse the input and return to us two values, symbol and price. These are specified as arguments to ReceiveStockPrice in the case statement; however, these are not passed in arguments. These are arguments that are passed out from the extractor. So, we're not sending the values for symbol and price. Instead, we are receiving them.

Let's take a look at the ReceiveStockPrice extractor. As you'd expect, it should have an unapply() that will split input over the : character and return a tuple of symbol and price. However, there is one catch; the input may not conform to the format "SYMBOL:PRICE." To handle this possibility, the return type of this method should be Option[(String, Double)], and at runtime we'll receive either Some(String, Double) or None.[1] Here's the code for the extractor ReceiveStockPrice:

PatternMatching/Extractor.scala

```
object ReceiveStockPrice {
  def unapply(input: String) : Option[(String, Double)] = {
    try {
      if (input contains ":") {
        val splitQuote = input split ":"
        Some(splitQuote(0), splitQuote(1).toDouble)
      }
      else {
        None
      }
    }
    catch {
      case _ : NumberFormatException => None
    }
  }
}
```

Here's how we might use the updated service:

PatternMatching/Extractor.scala

```
StockService process "GOOG"
StockService process "GOOG:310.84"
StockService process "GOOG:BUY"
StockService process "ERR:12.21"
```

---

1. See Section 5.4, *Option Type*, on page 60 for a discussion on Option[T], Some[T], and None.

The output from the previous code is shown here:

```
Look up price for valid symbol GOOG
Received price 310.840000 for symbol GOOG
Invalid input GOOG:BUY
Received price 12.210000 for symbol ERR
```

The code handled the first three requests well. It accepted what's valid and rejected what was not. The last request, however, did not go well. It should reject the request for invalid symbol ERR, even though the input was in a valid format. There are two ways we can handle that. One is to check whether the symbol is valid within ReceiveStockPrice. However, this will result in a duplication of effort. Alternately, we can apply multiple pattern matches in one case statement. Let's modify the process() method to do this:

```
case ReceiveStockPrice(symbol @ Symbol(), price) =>
  printf("Received price %f for symbol %s\n", price, symbol)
```

We first apply the ReceiveStockPrice extractor, which returns a pair of results if successful. On the first result (symbol), we further apply the Symbol extractor to validate the symbol. We can intercept this symbol on its way from one extractor to another using a pattern variable followed by the @ symbol, as shown in the previous code.

Now if we rerun the sample calls on this modified service, we'll get the following output:

```
Look up price for valid symbol GOOG
Received price 310.840000 for symbol GOOG
Invalid input GOOG:BUY
Invalid input ERR:12.21
```

You see how powerful extractors are. They allow you to match arbitrary patterns. You can pretty much take control of the matching in the unapply() method and return as many matching parts as you desire. Although this absolute power is very useful, if you can tailor your pattern into a regular expression, you don't have to go to those lengths to create a separate singleton extractor object. You'll see how to use regular expressions next.

9.9 Regular Expressions

Scala supports regular expressions[2] through classes in the scala.util.
matching package. When you create a regular expression, you're working with an instance of the Regex class in that package. Suppose we
want to check whether a given String contains either the word *Scala* or
the word *scala*:

PatternMatching/RegularExpr.scala

```
val pattern = "(S|s)cala".r
val str = "Scala is scalable and cool"
println(pattern findFirstIn str)
```

We create a String and call the r() method on it. Scala implicitly converts
the String to a RichString and invokes that method to get an instance of
Regex. Of course, if our regular expression needs escape characters,
we're better off using raw strings instead of strings. It's much easier to
write and read """\d2:\d2:\d4""" than "\\d2:\\d2:\\d4".

To find a first match of the regular expression, simply call the findFirstIn()
method. In the previous example, this will find the word Scala from the
given text.

If instead of finding only the first occurrence we'd like to find all occurrences of the matching word, we can use the findAllIn() method, as
shown here. This will return a collection of all matching words. In this
example, that would be (Scala, scala).

PatternMatching/RegularExpr.scala

```
println((pattern findAllIn str).mkString(", "))
```

In the previous code, we've concatenated the resulting list of elements
using the mkString() method.

If we'd like to replace matching text, we can use replaceFirstIn() to replace
the first match (as in the following example) or replaceAllIn() to replace
all occurrences:

PatternMatching/RegularExpr.scala

```
println("cool".r replaceFirstIn(str, "awesome"))
```

---

2. For a detailed discussion on regular expressions, refer to Jeffrey E. F. Friedl's *Mastering Regular Expressions* [Fri97].

The output from executing all three of the previous regular expression methods is shown here:

```
Some(Scala)
Scala, scala
Scala is scalable and awesome
```

If you're already familiar with regular expressions, using them in Scala is straightforward.

9.10 Regular Expressions as Extractors

Scala regular expressions offer a buy-one-get-one-free option. You create a regular expression, and you get an extractor for free. Scala regular expressions *are* extractors, so you can readily use them in case expressions. Scala rolls each match you place within parentheses into a pattern variable. So, for example, "(S|s)cala".r will hold an unapply() method that returns an Option[String]. On the other hand, "(S|s)(cala)".r's unapply() will return Option[String, String]. Let's explore this with an example. Suppose we want to pattern match "GOOG" stocks and get the price. Here is a way to do that using regular expressions:

PatternMatching/MatchUsingRegex.scala

```
def process(input : String) {
  val GoogStock = """^GOOG:(\d*\.\d+)""".r
  input match {
    case GoogStock(price) => println("Price of GOOG is " + price)
    case _ => println("not processing " + input)
  }
}

process("GOOG:310.84")
process("GOOG:310")
process("IBM:84.01")
```

We created a regular expression to match a string that starts with the "GOOG:" followed by a positive decimal number. We stored that in a val named GoogStock. Behind the scenes, Scala created an unapply() method for this extractor. It will return the value that matches the pattern within the parentheses—price:

```
Price of GOOG is 310.84
not processing GOOG:310
not processing IBM:84.01
```

The extractor we just created is not really reusable. It looks for the symbol "GOOG," but if we want to look for other symbols, that's not very useful. With hardly any effort, we can make it reusable:

```
def process(input : String) {
  val MatchStock = """^(.+):(\d*\.\d+)""".r
  input match {
    case MatchStock("GOOG", price) => println("Price of GOOG is " + price)
    case MatchStock("IBM", price) => println("IBM's trading at " + price)
    case MatchStock(symbol, price) => printf("Price of %s is %s\n", symbol, price)
    case _ => println("not processing " + input)
  }
}

process("GOOG:310.84")
process("IBM:84.01")
process("GE:15.96")
```

In the previous example, our regular expression matches a string that starts with any character or digit, followed by a colon and then a positive decimal number. The part before the : and the part after it are returned as two separate pattern variables by the generated unapply() method. We can match for specific stocks like GOOG and IBM, or we can simply receive whatever symbol that's given to us, as shown in the previous case expressions. The output from the previous code is shown here:

```
Price of GOOG is 310.84
IBM's trading at 84.01
Price of GE is 15.96
```

As you can see, Scala takes a no-sweat approach to using regular expressions in pattern matching.

In this chapter, you saw one of the most powerful features of Scala. Right off the shelf, you can match simple literals, types, tuples, lists, and so on. If you want a bit more control on the matching, you can use the case class or the all-too-charming extractors. You also saw how regular expressions manifest as extractors. If you want to match simple literals, the match is quite adequate. If you want to match arbitrary patterns, Scala extractors are your friend. Next you'll see how concurrent programming in Scala puts this feature to good use.

Chapter 10

Concurrent Programming

Scala makes it easy to implement multithreaded applications. In Java, you create a thread and then struggle to control it to avoid data contention using synchronization primitives, notifies, and waits.[1] Even then you question whether the code is right. Is there data contention or a possibility of deadlock lurking?

In Scala, you communicate between threads using an event-based model[2] to send immutable objects as messages. In this chapter, I'll introduce the concept of Scala's *actor* model. We'll use that together with all the concepts you have learned in this book to develop concurrent applications in Scala.

10.1 Promote Immutability

In the functional style of programming, you lean toward immutable objects. You can't modify the state of an immutable object once you create it. Although Java has immutable classes such as String, Class, and Integer, it's more common to use mutable objects and command query separation (see "Command Query Separation" in Appendix A, on page 207). You create an instance and invoke mutators or modifiers to change the state of the object. Let's spend a minute on why mutable objects are not desirable.

---

1. Full books, such as Doug Lea's *Concurrent Programming in Java* [Lea00] and Brian Goetz's *Java Concurrency in Practice* [Goe06], have been written on how to conquer threading in Java.
2. Scala's actor model is similar to Erlang's model. See Joe Armstrong's *Programming Erlang: Software for a Concurrent World* [Arm07] or Robert Virding et al.'s *Concurrent Programming in Erlang* [VWWA96].

In the following Java class, the Counter class has a field named count. That field can be accessed and modified using a getter and setter.

```java
//Java code
public class Counter {
  private int count;

  synchronized public int getCount() { return count; }
  synchronized public void setCount(int value) { count = value; }
}
```

In order to protect against multiple threads accessing the count, we have promptly *synchronized* the two methods. Unfortunately, this is not adequate. The following code is very problematic:

```java
//Java code
int currentValue = counter.getCount();
counter.setCount(currentValue + 100);
```

Suppose an instance of the Counter is used by multiple threads and each thread is performing an operation like in the previous example. The value of count is totally unpredictable. Even though both the methods of the Counter are synchronized, between the call to getCount() and the call to setCount() another thread may gain the monitor or lock and modify the value. This is an easy trap to fall into. We have to place the two calls within a proper synchronized block for the previous code to be thread safe. Furthermore, we have to check to make sure this is being done correctly at every place where the Counter is used. That is a tall order, and for any nontrivial application, it is extremely difficult, if not impossible, to write thread-safe code with mutable objects. This simple example is only the tip of the iceberg.

Immutable objects strike this problem at the root. Since there's no state to change, there's no contention to worry about. If you want to make a change, you simply create another instance of the immutable object. This may seem a bit strange if you're not used to functional programming. However, as you get comfortable with the style, you'll realize you're not facing the threading-related issues you currently fight. Immutable objects offer quite a few advantages:

- They are inherently thread safe. Since you can't modify their state, you can freely pass them between threads without fear of contention. There is no need to synchronize them.

- They are simple and easy to work with since they don't have a complicated state transition.

- They can be shared and reused across the application. This can help ease the burden on resources in your application. For example, in the Flyweight pattern,[3] immutable objects are used to share data that is common to several objects.

- They are less error prone. Since you do not arbitrarily modify the state of objects, you will have fewer errors to deal with. It is easier to verify the correctness of your code with immutable objects than with mutable objects.

Even in pure Java code, Joshua Bloch in *Effective Java* [Blo01] recommends that we "minimize mutability" and advocates making classes immutable as much as possible.

Scala's concurrency model depends on honoring immutability. Scala expects you to pass immutable objects as messages between actors. In the rest of this chapter, you will learn how Scala's support for concurrency is lightweight and quite easy to use compared to the concurrency API provided in Java.

10.2 Concurrency Using Actor

An actor in Scala provides an event-based lightweight thread. To create an actor, simply use the method named actor() in the scala.actors.Actor companion object. It accepts a function value/closure as a parameter and starts running as soon as you create it. If you want to send a message to an actor, use the !() method. To receive a message from an actor, use the receive() method. The receive() method accepts a closure as well, and typically you'd use pattern matching to process the received message.

Let's look at an example. Assume we need to determine whether a given number is a perfect number.[4]

ConcurrentProgramming/PerfectNumberFinder.scala

```
def sumOfFactors(number: Int) = {
  (0 /: (1 to number)) { (sum, i) => if (number % i == 0) sum + i else sum }
}

def isPerfect(candidate: Int) = 2 * candidate == sumOfFactors(candidate)
```

---

3. See the Flyweight pattern in Gamma et al.'s *Design Patterns: Elements of Reusable Object-Oriented Software* [GHJV95].

4. A perfect number is a positive integer whose factors add up to twice the number. For example, the first known perfect number is 6—its factors 1, 2, 3, 6 add up to 12.

This code computes the sum of factors for a given candidate number sequentially. This code has a problem. For large numbers, the sequential execution will be slow. Furthermore, if we were running this on a multicore processor, we would not be taking advantage of the additional cores. We let a single core do all the hard work, at any given instance, and have underutilized the other cores.

Let's exercise the previous code with a few sample numbers,[5] as shown here:

ConcurrentProgramming/PerfectNumberFinder.scala

```
println("6 is perfect? " + isPerfect(6))
println("33550336 is perfect? " + isPerfect(33550336))
println("33550337 is perfect? " + isPerfect(33550337))
```

The output from the previous code is shown here:

```
6 is perfect? true
33550336 is perfect? true
33550337 is perfect? false
```

On my machine, a MacBook Pro with a dual-core processor running Mac OS X, the two cores combined were utilized between 60 to 95 percent according to the Activity Monitor. The Activity Monitor reports maximum utilization capacity as 200 percent with two cores. So, a 95 percent utilization indicates only one core was being used effectively at any given instance for this computation-intensive operation. Or we could view it as the two cores being used at half their capacity.

By splitting the computation of the sum of factors to multiple threads, we can gain better throughput. Even on a single-processor machine, your application may receive more execution opportunity and be more responsive.

So, we can split the range of numbers from 1 to candidate into multiple partitions[6] and allocate the task of finding the sum for each partition to separate threads.

---

5. One of the technical reviewers tried to pass a very large number, close to scala.Math.MAX_INT, and ran into difficulties. Scala, just like Java, overflows when we exceed the limit. So, use caution, and check for overflows in your Scala code.
6. Choosing a partition granularity size, however, is tricky. It depends on at what point the increase in concurrency will offset any coordination overhead.

ConcurrentProgramming/FasterPerfectNumberFinder.scala

```
Line 1   import scala.actors.Actor._

    -    def sumOfFactorsInRange(lower: Int, upper: Int, number: Int) = {
    -      (0 /: (lower to upper)) { (sum, i) => if (number % i == 0) sum + i else sum }
    5    }

    -    def isPerfectConcurrent(candidate: Int) = {
    -      val RANGE = 1000000
    -      val numberOfPartitions = (candidate.toDouble / RANGE).ceil.toInt
    10     val caller = self

    -      for (i <- 0 until numberOfPartitions) {
    -        val lower = i * RANGE + 1;
    -        val upper = candidate min (i + 1) * RANGE
    15
    -        actor {
    -          caller ! sumOfFactorsInRange(lower, upper, candidate)
    -        }
    -      }
    20
    -      val sum = (0 /: (0 until numberOfPartitions)) { (partialSum, i) =>
    -        receive {
    -          case sumInRange : Int => partialSum + sumInRange
    -        }
    25     }

    -      2 * candidate == sum
    -    }

    30   println("6 is perfect? " + isPerfectConcurrent(6))
    -    println("33550336 is perfect? " + isPerfectConcurrent(33550336))
    -    println("33550337 is perfect? " + isPerfectConcurrent(33550337))
```

There is no synchronize or wait in the previous code. In the isPerfectConcurrent() method, we first partitioned the range of values. For each partition, we delegated the computation of the partial sum of factors to a separate actor in line number 16. When an actor completes its allocated task, it messages the partial sum to the caller on line number 17. The caller variable in this closure is bound to the variable in the isPerfectConcurrent() method—this variable holds a reference to the actor, obtained using a call to the self() method, that represents the main thread. Finally, we receive the messages from the delegated actors, one at a time, on line number 22. The foldLeft() method (shown here as method /:()) helps us receive all the partial sums and compute the total of those partial sums in functional style.

There wasn't much of a time difference between the two approaches. On my machine, the sequential program took about seven seconds, while the concurrent program took about five seconds. Since that is somewhat close, depending on other activities on the system, we may not be able to observe the difference. The Activity Monitor reported a 120 to 180 percent utilization in the second approach, which indicates more than one core being utilized at the same time. So, in order to make it a lot more obvious, let's find perfect numbers over a range of values:

ConcurrentProgramming/FindPerfectNumberOverRange.scala

```scala
def countPerfectNumbersInRange(start : Int, end : Int,
  isPerfectFinder : Int => Boolean) = {

  val startTime = System.nanoTime()
  val numberOfPerfectNumbers = (0 /: (start to end)) { (count, candidate) =>
    if (isPerfectFinder(candidate)) count + 1 else count
  }
  val endTime = System.nanoTime()

  println("Found " + numberOfPerfectNumbers +
    " perfect numbers in given range, took " +
    (endTime - startTime)/1000000000.0 + " secs")
}

val startNumber = 33550300
val endNumber = 33550400
countPerfectNumbersInRange(startNumber, endNumber, isPerfect)
countPerfectNumbersInRange(startNumber, endNumber, isPerfectConcurrent)
```

In countPerfectNumbersInRange(), we count the number of perfect numbers in the given range from start to end. The actual method to find out whether a candidate number is a perfect number is delegated to the closure, isPerfectFinder, received as a parameter. The time it takes to find the number of perfect numbers in the given range is computed using the JDK System.nanoTime() method. We then invoke the countPerfectNumbersInRange() twice, first using the sequential implementation isPerfect() and second using the concurrent implementation isPerfectConcurrent().

The output from the previous code is shown here:

```
Found 1 perfect numbers in given range, took 322.681763 secs
Found 1 perfect numbers in given range, took 219.511014 secs
```

This time the sequential computation took nearly two minutes more than the concurrent implementation to determine the number of perfect numbers in a range of 100 values starting from 33,550,300.

10.3 Message Passing

Next let's look at how messages get from one actor to another. Each actor has its own message queue—it receives input from an InputChannel[Any] and sends output through an OutputChannel[Any].

Imagine that each actor is using a phone-answering service. There are calls coming in while the actor is away or unable to answer the phone. The missed calls may be friends inviting our actor to parties as well as reminder messages the actor sends to himself. These are all stored in his voice mail sequentially, and he can retrieve them one at a time at his convenience. Similarly, the actors leave messages for one another. An actor is not blocked when it sends a message. An actor is, however, blocked if it calls the receive() method. On the other hand, an actor that is busy is not interrupted by a message. Let's understand these concepts with an example:

ConcurrentProgramming/MessagePassing.scala

```scala
import scala.actors.Actor._

var startTime : Long = 0
val caller = self

val engrossedActor = actor {
  println("Number of messages received so far? " + mailboxSize)
  caller ! "send"
  Thread.sleep(3000)
  println("Number of messages received while I was busy? " + mailboxSize)
  receive {
    case msg =>
      val receivedTime = System.currentTimeMillis() - startTime
      println("Received message " + msg + " after " + receivedTime + " ms")
  }
  caller ! "received"
}

receive { case _ => }

println("Sending Message ")
startTime = System.currentTimeMillis()
engrossedActor ! "hello buddy"
val endTime = System.currentTimeMillis() - startTime

printf("Took less than %dms to send message\n", endTime)

receive {
  case _ =>
}
```

The output from the previous code is shown here:

```
Number of messages received so far? 0
Sending Message
Took less than 1ms to send message
Number of messages received while I was busy? 1
Received message hello buddy after 3002 ms
```

From the output you see that the send did not block and the receive did not interrupt. The message was waiting for the receiving actor until it called the receive() method.

Sending and receiving messages asynchronously is a good practice—you can make the most use of concurrency. However, if you are interested in sending a message and receiving a response synchronously, you can use the !?() method. This will block until it receives a response from the actor to which you sent the message. This may lead to a potential deadlock. A failed actor may lead to failure of other actors and in turn your application. So if you need to use this method, you may want to at least use the variation that takes a timeout as a parameter like this:

ConcurrentProgramming/AskFortune.scala

```scala
import scala.actors._
import Actor._

val fortuneTeller = actor {
  for (i <- 1 to 4) {
    Thread.sleep(1000)
    receive {
      case _ => sender ! "your day will rock! " + i
      //case _ => reply("your day will rock! " + i) // same as above
    }
  }
}

println( fortuneTeller !? (2000, "what's ahead") )
println( fortuneTeller !? (500, "what's ahead") )

val aPrinter = actor {
  receive { case msg => println("Ah, fortune message for you-" + msg) }
}

fortuneTeller.send("What's up", aPrinter)

fortuneTeller ! "How's my future?"

Thread.sleep(3000)
```

```
receive { case msg : String => println("Received " + msg ) }

println("Let's get that lost message")
receive { case !(channel, msg) => println("Received belated message " + msg) }
```

The !?() method will return the result if the actor sends it a message before the timeout. Otherwise, it has to return None, so this method's return type is Option[Any].[7] In the previous code we used sender to reference the actor that sent us the last message. Alternately, we may use the reply() method to implicitly send the message to the last sender. We can alter the sender, if we desire. Suppose we want to send a message to an actor, but we want it to forward the result to some other actor (like aPrinter in the previous example). We can use the send() method. In this case, the reply is sent to the delegate we assign instead of the real caller. You may wonder what happened to the message that we did not receive when we bailed out of the call to !?() because of a timeout. That message was eventually received by your actor, and it sent a message to itself to help process that message later. We can retrieve that message using a special case class:[8] ![a](val ch : Channel[a], val msg : a). This case class represents messages sent by an actor to itself. So, while we continue to process other messages, if we are interested in processing missed messages, we can use this case class to fetch it, as shown in the last line of the previous code.

The output from the previous code is shown here:

```
Some(your day will rock! 1)
None
Ah, fortune message for you-your day will rock! 3
Received your day will rock! 4
Let's get that lost message
Received belated message your day will rock! 2
```

Now that you have a basic understanding of how actors interact, let's dig a little deeper.

10.4 The Actor Class

In the previous example we used the actor() method of the Actor singleton object. That is all you need most of the time. However, if you want

---

7. See Section 5.4, *Option Type*, on page 60 for details on the Option type.
8. For a discussion of case classes, see Section 9.7, *Matching Using case Classes*, on page 114.

to have explicit control over when an actor is started and want to store more information within an actor, you can create an object that has the Actor trait. That's right—Scala's Actor is simply a trait, and you can mix it in wherever you like. Here's an example:

ConcurrentProgramming/AnsweringService.scala
```
import scala.actors._
import Actor._

class AnsweringService(val folks: String*) extends Actor {
  def act() {
    while(true) {
      receive {
        case (caller : Actor, name : String, msg : String) =>
          caller ! (
          if(folks.contains(name))
            String.format("Hey it's %s got message %s", name,  msg)
          else
            String.format("Hey there's no one with the name %s here", name)
          )
        case "ping" => println("ping!")
        case "quit" => println("exiting actor")
          exit
      }
    }
  }
}
```

We create a class AnsweringService that mixes in the trait Actor; remember, if you don't extend any class, you use the keyword extends to mix in a trait (see Section 7.1, *Traits*, on page 83). Our AnsweringService receives an array of recognized names as the constructor parameter. We implement the required act() method in our class (this method is abstract in the Actor trait). Within this method, we process three types of messages: a tuple and two literals, "ping" and "quit":

ConcurrentProgramming/AnsweringService.scala
```
val answeringService1 = new AnsweringService("Sara", "Kara", "John")

answeringService1 ! (self, "Sara", "In town")
answeringService1 ! (self, "Kara", "Go shopping?")

answeringService1.start()

answeringService1 ! (self, "John", "Bug fixed?")
answeringService1 ! (self, "Bill", "What's up")

for(i <- 1 to 4) { receive { case msg => println(msg) }  }
```

```
answeringService1 ! "ping"
answeringService1 ! "quit"
answeringService1 ! "ping"

Thread.sleep(2000)
println("The last ping was not processed")
```

The output from the previous code is shown here:

```
Hey it's Sara got message In town
Hey it's Kara got message Go shopping?
Hey it's John got message Bug fixed?
Hey there's no one with the name Bill here
ping!
exiting actor
The last ping was not processed
```

We send a couple of tuple messages to the actor to begin with. These messages will not be processed right away because we did not start the actor yet. They're queued for later processing. We then call the start() method and send a couple of more messages. As soon as we called the start() method, the act() method of the actor was called in a separate thread. The messages we have sent so far are now processed. We then loop through and receive the response to the four messages we've sent so far.

You can stop the actor by calling the exit() method. However, this method simply throws an exception in an attempt to terminate the current thread of execution, so a good place to call it is within the act() method. A variation of this method takes a reason for exiting as a parameter; use it if you care to send a reason. In the previous code, upon receiving the "quit" message, we call the exit() method to terminate the execution of this actor. The "ping" message we sent before sending the "quit" message was processed. However, the one we sent after was not. You can see this from the output shown. Any message sent to the actor after the call to exit() is simply queued. You can restart the actor, if you like, by calling the start() method. It will then start processing any queued messages and then process messages received.

10.5 The actor Method

In the previous example, we controlled when the actor was started. If you don't really care about explicitly staring an actor, then the actor() method is the way to go. You can pass data between the actors using the !() and receive() methods. Let's start with an example of using the actor() method and then refactor it to make it concurrent.

Here is a method (isPrime()) that tells us whether a given number is prime. For illustrative purposes, I have some added print statements in this method:

ConcurrentProgramming/PrimeTeller.scala

```scala
import scala.actors._
import Actor._

def isPrime(number: Int) = {
  println("Going to find if " + number + " is prime")

  var result = true

  if (number == 2 || number == 3) result = true

  for (i <- 2 to Math.sqrt(number.toDouble).floor.toInt; if result) {
    if (number % i == 0) result = false
  }

  println("done finding if " + number + " is prime")
  result
}
```

If we call the previous method, we will be blocked until we receive a response. Let's delegate the responsibility of calling this method to an actor, as shown here. This actor will determine whether a number is prime and send an asynchronous response back to the caller.

ConcurrentProgramming/PrimeTeller.scala

```scala
Line 1   val primeTeller = actor {
     2     var continue = true
     3
     4     while (continue) {
     5       receive {
     6         case (caller : Actor, number: Int) => caller ! (number, isPrime(number))
     7         case "quit" => continue = false
     8       }
     9     }
    10   }
```

primeTeller is a reference to an anonymous actor created using the actor() method. It loops through until it receives a "quit" message. Other than the message to quit, it can also receive a tuple of caller and a number. Upon receiving this message, it finds out whether the given number is prime and sends back a message to the caller.

Let's ask this actor to find out whether three arbitrary numbers (2, 131, 132) are prime:

ConcurrentProgramming/PrimeTeller.scala

```
primeTeller ! (self, 2)
primeTeller ! (self, 131)
primeTeller ! (self, 132)

for (i <- 1 to 3) {
  receive {
    case (number, result) => println(number + " is prime? " + result)
  }
}
```

```
primeTeller ! "quit"
```

The previous example processes each number as it is received; you can see that from the following output. The multiple requests received while the actor is busy finding out whether a number is prime are queued. So, the execution is sequential even though we delegated it to an actor.

```
Going to find if 2 is prime
done finding if 2 is prime
2 is prime? true
Going to find if 131 is prime
done finding if 131 is prime
Going to find if 132 is prime
131 is prime? true
done finding if 132 is prime
132 is prime? false
```

Fear not, we can quite easily make this example concurrent so it can process multiple requests for prime numbers at the same time. On line number 6 in the primeTeller actor, instead of calling the isPrime() method, delegate that responsibility to another actor and have him forward the response to your caller:

```
//case (caller : Actor, number: Int) => caller ! (number, isPrime(number))
case (caller : Actor, number: Int) => actor { caller ! (number, isPrime(number)) }
```

If we run the code again with the previous change, you'll notice that multiple calls to isPrime() are executed concurrently, as shown here:

```
Going to find if 131 is prime
Going to find if 2 is prime
Going to find if 132 is prime
done finding if 2 is prime
done finding if 131 is prime
2 is prime? true
131 is prime? true
done finding if 132 is prime
132 is prime? false
```

You can write concurrent code effortlessly and in a thread-safe manner. Remember, the key to success here is immutable objects. Nowhere did we share a common state in objects between threads—I mean actors.

One other observation from the previous output—there is no guarantee of the ordering of interaction with the actors. Actors will process messages as they are received and respond as soon as they're ready. There is no pre-imposed order on which messages are received and processed by an actor.

10.6 receive and receiveWithin Methods

The receive() method accepts a function value/closure and returns a response of the processed message. Here's an example of receiving results from the receive() method:

ConcurrentProgramming/Receive.scala

```
import scala.actors.Actor._

val caller = self

val accumulator = actor {
  var sum = 0
  var continue = true
  while (continue) {
    sum += receive {
      case number : Int => number
      case "quit" =>
        continue = false
        0
    }
  }

  caller ! sum
}

accumulator ! 1
accumulator ! 7
accumulator ! 8
accumulator ! "quit"

receive { case result => println("Total is " + result) }
```

The accumulator receives and totals the numbers sent to it. When done, it sends back a message with the sum. The output from the previous code is shown here:

```
Total is 16
```

This code shows that even though receive() has special significance, it's just another method. However, the code is blocked when we call receive() until a response is actually received. This is not good news if the actor from which we're expecting a response is not going to send us one. This would leave us waiting forever—a liveness failure—and make us quite unpopular among colleagues. We can fix that by using the receiveWithin() method, which takes a timeout, as shown here:

`ConcurrentProgramming/ReceiveWithin.scala`

```
import scala.actors._
import scala.actors.Actor._

val caller = self

val accumulator = actor {
  var sum = 0
  var continue = true
  while (continue) {
    sum += receiveWithin(1000) {
      case number : Int => number
      case TIMEOUT =>
        println("Timed out! Will return result now")
        continue = false
        0
    }
  }

  caller ! sum
}

accumulator ! 1
accumulator ! 7
accumulator ! 8

receiveWithin(10000) { case result => println("Total is " + result) }
```

If nothing is received within the given timeout period, the receiveWithin() method receives a TIMEOUT message. If we don't pattern match it, an exception is thrown. In the previous code, we took the receipt of the TIMEOUT message as a signal that we're done with accumulating values. The output from the previous code is shown here:

```
Timed out! Will return result now
Total is 16
```

You should prefer using the receiveWithin() method to the receive() method to avoid the liveness problem.

Oh, one last thing about receive() and receiveWithin()—they're quite diligent, and they don't waste any time on messages they don't care about. This is because these methods treat the function value as partially applied functions and check whether it handles the message before calling the code block. So, if a message received is not what you expect, it's quietly ignored. Of course, if you want to complain about it, you can always provide a case _ => .... Here's an example that shows that invalid messages are ignored:

```
ConcurrentProgramming/MessageIgnore.scala
import scala.actors._
import Actor._

val expectStringOrInteger = actor {
  for(i <- 1 to 4) {
    receiveWithin(1000) {
      case str : String => println("You said " + str)
      case num : Int => println("You gave " + num)
      case TIMEOUT => println("Timed out!")
    }
  }
}

expectStringOrInteger ! "only constant is change"
expectStringOrInteger ! 1024
expectStringOrInteger ! 22.22
expectStringOrInteger ! (self, 1024)

receiveWithin(3000) { case _ => }
```

At the end of the previous code, we placed a call to receiveWithin(). Since the program quits when the main thread quits, this statement will keep the program alive, giving the actor a chance to respond. You can see from the output that the actor processed the first two messages sent to it and ignored the remaining two since they did not match the pattern of the message it expected. It eventually timed out since it did not receive any more messages that it matched with.

```
You said only constant is change
You gave 1024
Timed out!
Timed out!
```

10.7 react and reactWithin Methods

You saw how to avoid the problem of contention by passing immutable objects between actors. There is one problem that still needs to be solved. In each actor, when you called receive(), you actually asked for a separate thread. You will hold on to that thread until you're done with that actor completely. That means, even though you are waiting for messages to arrive, you will be holding on to those threads, one per actor, and that's a waste of resources.

The reason Scala has to hold on to those threads is that there is state that is specific to the control flow of execution. If there were no state to be retained and returned in that call sequence, then Scala could pretty much get any thread from the thread pool to execute your message handling—that's exactly what happens when you use react().

Unlike its cousin receive(), the react() method does not return any results. In fact, it never returns from the call you make to it. When you complete a call to receive(), the code that follows the call is executed (as with any typical function call). However, when you call react(), any code you place after the call is unreachable. This may be a bit confusing, but it gets easier if you look at this a bit differently. When you call react(), imagine that the thread that called it is released immediately (the underlying implementation is quite complex, but Scala achieves this behavior by the react() method throwing an exception internally and the calling thread handling it). When you receive a message that matches one of the case statements within the react() method, a thread from a thread pool is assigned to execute the body of that case. It continues to run until it hits another call to react() or has no more code to execute within the case statement. At which point, the thread returns to processing other messages or to doing whatever other tasks are assigned to it by the virtual machine.

If you want to continue processing more messages after you process the current message within react(), you'd have to call other methods at the end of your message processing. Scala can pretty much hand over the execution of that call to any thread from the thread pool. Let's take a look at this behavior with an example:

`ConcurrentProgramming/React.scala`

```
import scala.actors.Actor._

def info(msg: String) = println(msg + " received by " + Thread.currentThread())

def receiveMessage(id : Int) {
  for(i <- 1 to 2) {
      receiveWithin(20000) {
        case msg : String => info("receive: " + id + msg) }
  }
}
```

```
def reactMessage(id : Int) {
  react {
    case msg : String => info("react:    " + id + msg)
    reactMessage(id)
  }
}

val actors = Array(
  actor { info("react:    1 actor created"); reactMessage(1) },
  actor { info("react:    2 actor created"); reactMessage(2) },
  actor { info("receive: 3 actor created"); receiveMessage(3) },
  actor { info("receive: 4 actor created"); receiveMessage(4) }
  )

Thread.sleep(1000)
for(i <- 0 to 3) { actors(i) ! " hello"; Thread.sleep(2000) }
Thread.sleep(2000)
for(i <- 0 to 3) { actors(i) ! " hello"; Thread.sleep(2000) }
```

Here, receiveMessage() uses the receiveWithin() method to process the
messages that arrive. In this case we're in an active loop and will get
more messages. On the other hand, reactMessage() uses the react()
methods and is not in a while or a for loop—instead, it calls itself recursively at the end.

We've created four actors, two that use react() and two that use receive-
Within(). Finally, we send a series of messages to these four actors at
rather a slow pace. Each actor will report the message it receives along
with the thread that executes it.

The output from the previous code is shown here:

```
react:    2 actor created received by Thread[Thread-4,5,main]
receive: 3 actor created received by Thread[Thread-6,5,main]
react:    1 actor created received by Thread[Thread-3,5,main]
receive: 4 actor created received by Thread[Thread-5,5,main]
react:    1 hello received by Thread[Thread-3,5,main]
react:    2 hello received by Thread[Thread-3,5,main]
receive: 3 hello received by Thread[Thread-6,5,main]
receive: 4 hello received by Thread[Thread-5,5,main]
react:    1 hello received by Thread[Thread-4,5,main]
react:    2 hello received by Thread[Thread-3,5,main]
receive: 3 hello received by Thread[Thread-6,5,main]
receive: 4 hello received by Thread[Thread-5,5,main]
```

The actors that use the receiveWithin() method have thread affinity; they
continue to use the same thread they're assigned. In the previous output, receive: 3 is always handled by Thread-6 and receive: 4 by Thread-5.

On the other hand, the actors using react() are freely swapping their threads, being picked up by any available thread. In the previous output, the actor using react: 1 was originally executed by Thread-3. This same thread happens to execute the first message processing for this actor. However, the second message this actor received was handled by a different thread, Thread-4. This latter thread is the one that handled the creation of the actor using react: 2. However, the two subsequent messages for this actor are handled by Thread-3.

In other words, the actors using react() don't have any thread affinity; they let go of their thread, and a new one (or the same one) can pick up subsequent message processing. This will be kinder on your resources, especially when the message handling is fairly quick. So, there is a good incentive to use react() over receive(). Because of the nondeterministic nature of threads, when you run the previous code, you may observe a different output sequence than I have. Play with it by running it several times.

There is one smell in the previous code. We have to remember to call an appropriate method at the end of processing messages in the react() method call. If we forget, no more messages will be processed by this actor. However, writing that call is not elegant, and we could easily forget to write it. It gets only more complicated if we have multiple case statements within the react() call. We may have to call the method in each of the case branches. Fortunately, there is a better way to handle this, as you'll see in Section 10.8, *loop and loopWhile*, on page 145.

Similar to receiveWithin(), reactWithin() will time out if any message is not received within the timeout period—in this case, if you handle case TIME-OUT, you can take whatever action you want or exit from the method. As an example of using reactWithin(), let's take a stab at the accumulator examples we implemented earlier using receiveWithin(), this time using the reactWithin() method:

`ConcurrentProgramming/ReactWithin.scala`

```
import scala.actors._
import Actor._

val caller = self

def accumulate() {
  var sum = 0
  reactWithin(500) {
    case number: Int => sum += number
    accumulate()
```

```
      case TIMEOUT =>
        println("Timed out! Will send result now")
        caller ! sum
    }
    println("This will not be called...")
}

val accumulator = actor { accumulate() }
accumulator ! 1
accumulator ! 7
accumulator ! 8

receiveWithin(10000) { case result => println("Total is " + result) }
```

The output from the previous code is shown here:

```
Timed out! Will send result now
Total is 0
```

The output is not quite what we'd like to see. Let's analyze this and then fix the problem. Since reactWithin() will not return any value, we can't do any processing in the accumulate() method outside of the call to reactWithin(). So, we decided to add to the local variable sum from within the closure attached to the call to reactWithin(). Unfortunately, when we call accumulate() within the case statement, the value of sum is different within the new call because it is local to each method call. So, the value of sum in each call to accumulate() starts with a zero. But don't worry, there is an easy fix for this. While fixing the problem on hand, we will make the code more functional as well, so we don't have to modify the variable sum.

Let's modify our example to fix the problem:

ConcurrentProgramming/ReactWithin2.scala

```
import scala.actors._
import Actor._

val caller = self

def accumulate(sum : Int) {
  reactWithin(500) {
    case number: Int => accumulate(sum + number)
    case TIMEOUT =>
      println("Timed out! Will send result now")
      caller ! sum
  }
  println("This will not be called...")
}
```

```
val accumulator = actor { accumulate(0) }
accumulator ! 1
accumulator ! 7
accumulator ! 8

receiveWithin(10000) { case result => println("Total is " + result) }
```

We turned the sum, which was a local variable, into a function parameter. Now we don't have to modify an existing variable. Each call to accumulate() gets a good value of sum. A new value of sum is computed without changing any variables and passed on to the next call to accumulate() until timeout. Finally, on timeout, the current value of sum is sent to the caller.

The output from the previous code is shown here:

```
Timed out! Will send result now
Total is 16
```

This solution is more elegant than the solution using receiveWithin(), and it also does not hold any threads while waiting to receive a message.

One final point to remember about react() and reactWithin() is that since these two methods do not really return from the call (remember that internally Scala handles this by having these methods throw an exception), any code you place after the call to these methods will never get executed[9] (like the print statement at the end of the accumulate() method). So, don't bother writing anything after a call to either of these two methods.

10.8 loop and loopWhile

There are two things that stand in your way to fully use react() and reactWithin(). (In rest of this section, when I speak about reactWithin(), the discussion applies to react() also.) The first is the recursive call. If you have multiple case statements, and typically you would, you'd have to duplicate the call in each case. Second, there seems to be no good way to bail out of the method. The answer to the first concern is the loop() method of the singleton Actor class, and the answer to the second is the loopWhile() method.

Instead of calling methods recursively within reactWithin(), place the call to reactWithin() inside a loop() call. The thread executing the loop()

---

9. It would be nice if Scala gave an unreachable error for this.

method will relinquish control when it hits the call to reactWithin(). When the message arrives, an arbitrary thread will pick up the execution of an appropriate case statement. When the case statement is completed, the thread will continue back at the top of the loop() block. This continues forever. The loopWhile() method is similar, except the looping continues only as long as the condition you present as a parameter is valid. Since the loopWhile() is taking care of the looping, you can put local state outside the loop and access it within the reactWithin() method. So, this gives the best of both worlds, dealing with state as provided by receiveWithin() and utilizing threads from a pool as reactWithin(). Let's take a look at an example of using reactWithin() within a loopWhile():

ConcurrentProgramming/Loop.scala

```scala
import scala.actors._
import Actor._

val caller = self

val accumulator = actor {
  var continue = true
  var sum = 0

  loopWhile(continue) {
    reactWithin(500) {
      case number : Int => sum += number
      case TIMEOUT =>
        continue = false
        caller ! sum
    }
  }
}

accumulator ! 1
accumulator ! 7
accumulator ! 8

receiveWithin(1000) { case result => println("Total is " + result) }
```

In the previous code, we're not making any recursive calls—that's taken care of by the loopWhile(). Also, when we want to quit processing messages, simply set the flag, and it takes care of quitting from the loop and hence the actor execution. The output from the previous code is shown here:

```
Total is 16
```

10.9 Controlling Thread of Execution

You saw how each actor runs in its own thread when you use receive and how react lets the actors share threads from the thread pool. There are times, however, when you want more control. For instance, if you want to update a UI after a long-running task, you'd want to run the task in a separate thread but then update the UI from the main thread (because UI components are often not thread safe). You can tell Scala to run an actor in the main thread by using SingleThreadedScheduler. Let's see how with an example:

ConcurrentProgramming/InMainThread.scala

```scala
import scala.actors._
import Actor._

if (args.length > 0 && args(0) == "Single") {
  println("Command-line argument Single found")
  Scheduler.impl = new SingleThreadedScheduler
}

println("Main running in " + Thread.currentThread)

actor { println("Actor1 running in " + Thread.currentThread) }

actor { println("Actor2 running in " + Thread.currentThread) }

receiveWithin(3000) { case _ => }
```

In the previous code, we create two actors. If we do not send any command-line arguments, the code in the two actors and the code in the main script run in their own threads, as shown in the following output:

```
Main running in Thread[main,5,main]
Actor2 running in Thread[Thread-5,5,main]
Actor1 running in Thread[Thread-3,5,main]
```

On the other hand, if we run the previous code as scala InMainThread. scala Single, we get a different result:

```
Command-line argument Single found
Main running in Thread[main,5,main]
Actor1 running in Thread[main,5,main]
Actor2 running in Thread[main,5,main]
```

Whenever an actor is started, Scala lets the singleton Scheduler run it. By setting the Scheduler's impl, you can control the actors' scheduling strategy for your entire application.

The previous approach is far-reaching; it allowed us to control the scheduling of *all* actors. However, you may want to let some actors run in the main thread and let other actors run in their own threads. You can do that by extending the Actor trait and overriding the scheduler() method. By default, this method returns the singleton Scheduler for an actor to be scheduled. By overriding this method, you can control how individual actors are scheduled, as shown here:

ConcurrentProgramming/InMainThreadSelective.scala

```
import scala.actors._
import Actor._

trait SingleThreadedActor extends Actor {
  override protected def scheduler() = new SingleThreadedScheduler
}

class MyActor1 extends Actor {
  def act() = println("Actor1 running in " + Thread.currentThread)
}

class MyActor2 extends SingleThreadedActor {
  def act() = println("Actor2 running in " + Thread.currentThread)
}

println("Main running in " + Thread.currentThread)
new MyActor1().start()
new MyActor2().start()
actor { println("Actor 3 running in " + Thread.currentThread) }

receiveWithin(5000) { case _ => }
```

In the previous code, we've created three actors, two by extending the Actor trait and one using the more convenient actor() method. We control the thread of MyActor2 by overriding the protected method scheduler(). When we run the previous code, the actors created using the actor() method and MyActor1 run in their own threads. However, the actor created using MyActor2 runs in the main thread, as shown here:

```
Main running in Thread[main,5,main]
Actor1 running in Thread[Thread-2,5,main]
Actor2 running in Thread[main,5,main]
Actor 3 running in Thread[Thread-4,5,main]
```

10.10 Choosing Among the Receive Methods

It can get overwhelming when you're presented with several options, so in this section I will help you decide which method to use among receive(), receiveWithin(), react(), and reactWithin().

You should prefer the methods ending with *Within* over the other methods. Calling receive() or react() can lead to a failure. Your actor may end up waiting forever for a response that it may never receive because the actor that was supposed to send the message has quit, has run into problems and will no longer send a message, or has performed an invalid operation resulting in a fatal exception. So, certainly you should prefer using either receiveWithin() or reactWithin() so you can gracefully recover from getting no response within a reasonable amount of time and take an appropriate action.

So, when should you use receiveWithin(), and when should you use reactWithin()? If in the middle of an execution of a workflow you want to receive a message from another actor, then receiveWithin() is quite suitable. Your actor will be blocked until you receive the message and can continue upon receipt. You don't want to have too many of these actors since each one of them holds a separate thread until completion. On the other hand, if you are implementing a service that receives a message, does some operation, and quickly responds to the caller (or another receiver), then you are better off using reactWithin(). While waiting for a message to arrive, you're not holding a thread. This allows several quick-running tasks or services to share the threads. If you're in doubt, try using reactWithin() and escalate to using receiveWithin() only if reactWithin() will not serve your needs. You need to remember to call reactWithin() from within loopWhile() so your actor can continue to process more messages. This will also help you deal with state within your actor if you desire. If you prefer a more functional style, you can recursively call your method from within reactWithin() as well. The latter approach is OK if you have one or two case statements in your reactWithin().

I hope you've ended this chapter as impressed with Scala's facility for concurrent programming as I. You have an amazing amount of power and don't have to endure synchronization and exceptions. As long as you're a good citizen—that is, you pass around only immutable objects—you don't have to worry about contention. Scala's higher level of abstraction helps you focus on the problem at hand and leave it to the language to deal with those mundane details. The result is concise code with fewer bugs to deal with in this highly critical and complex area.

You can build your entire application in Scala or build parts of the application with Scala—Scala gives you the flexibility to choose. If you have a legacy Java application and decide to take advantage of Scala for its expressiveness, conciseness, power, or concurrency support, you can easily intermix Scala with Java, as you'll see in the next chapter.

Chapter 11

Intermixing with Java

In this chapter, you'll learn how to use Java classes in Scala and use Scala classes in Java. You can easily intermix Scala code with code written in Java and other languages on the JVM. Scala compiles into bytecode just like Java. This allows you to use that bytecode in your application like you use the bytecode compiled with Java. You simply make sure that scala-library.jar is in your classpath, and you're all set.

We'll discuss how Scala idioms manifest on the Java side. So, you can readily put the Scala strengths like concurrency, pattern matching, functional style, and conciseness in your current Java applications. At the end of this chapter, you'll be equipped with what you need to take full advantage of Scala in your Java applications.

11.1 Using Scala Classes in Scala

Before we talk about mixing Java and Scala, let's look at using Scala classes from Scala. If you've created Scala classes in separate files, you can readily use those classes as is (without explicitly compiling) from within Scala scripts.[1] However, if you want to use a Scala class from within compiled Scala or Java code, you have to compile it.

---

1. See Section 2.4, *Scala on the Command Line*, on page 21 for details on how to run Scala code as a script.

Suppose we have Scala classes named Person and Dog. In general, it is a good practice to place each class in its own file. I've combined them both in the Person.scala file to make a point:

WorkingWithScriptsAndClasses/Person.scala
```
class Person(val firstName: String, val lastName: String) {
  override def toString() : String = firstName + " " + lastName
}

class Dog(name: String) {
  override def toString() :String = name
}
```

Here's a script that uses both of the previous classes:

WorkingWithScriptsAndClasses/usePerson.scala
```
val george = new Person("George", "Washington")

val georgesDogs = List(new Dog("Captain"), new Dog("Clode"),
  new Dog("Forester"), new Dog("Searcher"))

printf("%s had several dogs %s...", george, georgesDogs mkString ", ")
```

The script will generate this:

```
George Washington had several dogs Captain, Clode, Forester, Searcher...
```

We did not have to compile any of the previous code. When we referred to the class Person, Scala looked for a file named Person.scala and loaded it. Since that file also contains Dog, that class got resolved as well. Instead, if we had the Dog class in its own separate file Dog.scala or we had a compiled bytecode file named Dog.class, Scala would have picked up the Dog class from there. However, if the Dog class were in some other arbitrary file, Scala would have trouble finding it.

In the previous example, both the files Person.scala and usePerson.scala were in the same directory. Suppose the file Person.scala is in a different directory, such as entities. We can specify that directory in the sourcepath option to the scala tool as follows:

```
scala -sourcepath entities:. usePerson.scala
```

If the class is in a compiled form in a different directory, use the classpath option instead or in addition to the sourcepath option.

You saw how to use Scala classes in scripts. However, to use them in other Scala classes, we'll have to first compile them.

Suppose we want to use the previous Person class in the following Scala code:

WorkingWithScriptsAndClasses/UsePersonClass.scala

```
object UsePersonClass {
  def main(args: Array[String]) {
    val ben = new Person("Ben", "Franklin")

    println(ben + " was a great inventor.")
  }
}
```

If the Person class has already been compiled, we can simply compile the UsePersonClass.scala file alone. If the Person.class is not located in the current directory, use the classpath option—the -d option tells where to put the bytecode:

```
scalac -d . -classpath LocationOfPersonClassFile UsePersonClass.scala
```

On the other hand, if the Person class is not already compiled, we can compile it alongside UsePersonClass. Specify the sourcepath so the compiler can find the files it needs to compile alongside. So, use the following:

```
scalac -sourcepath LocationOfPersonScalaFile:. UsePersonClass.scala
```

where LocationOfPersonScalaFile is the location of the Person.scala file. Alternately, use scalac -sourcepath . UsePersonClass.scala if all the related files are in the current directory. Of course, you can use both the sourcepath and the classpath options—this will allow you to pick up Scala source files and compiled bytecode from any language on the JVM (Java, Groovy, JRuby, Scala, and so on).

You can run the compiled bytecode either using the scala tool or using the traditional java tool. Here's an example of using the scala tool[2] to run the UsePersonClass.class file:

```
scalac -sourcepath . UsePersonClass.scala
scala UsePersonClass
```

On the other hand, if you want to run it using java tool, simply specify the scala-library.jar file in the classpath (make sure to use the correct path to scala-library.jar on your machine):

```
scalac -sourcepath . UsePersonClass.scala
java -classpath /opt/scala/scala-2.7.4.final/lib/scala-library.jar:. UsePersonClass
```

---

2. You can use the scala tool to run both Scala compiled code and code compiled using javac.

You can see here that both of the previous approaches will yield the same result:

```
Ben Franklin was a great inventor.
```

11.2 Using Java Classes in Scala

Using Java classes from Scala is pretty straightforward. If the Java class you'd like to use is part of the standard JDK, then simply use it. You'll have to import the class's package if it's not part of java.lang. Here, we use classes from the java.util and java.lang.reflect packages:

WorkingWithScriptsAndClasses/UseJDKClasses.scala

```scala
import java.util.Date
import java.lang.reflect._

println("Today is " + new Date())

val methods = getClass.getMethods()
methods.foreach { method: Method => println(method.getName()) }
```

If the Java class you'd like to use is your own or from a third party, make sure to specify to scalac the classpath to where the bytecode is located. Suppose we have the following Java files:

WorkingWithScriptsAndClasses/InvestmentType.java

```java
//Java code
package investments;

public enum InvestmentType {
  SHORT_TERM,
  BOND,
  STOCK,
  REAL_ESTATE,
  COMMODITIES,
  COLLECTIBLES,
  MUTUAL_FUNDS
}
```

WorkingWithScriptsAndClasses/Investment.java

```java
//Java code
package investments;

public class Investment {
  private String investmentName;
  private InvestmentType investmentType;

  public Investment(String name, InvestmentType type) {
    investmentName = name;
```

```
      investmentType = type;
   }

   public int yield() { return 0; }
}
```

We can use these classes in our Scala code just like we use any Scala class. Here's an example of creating an instance of Investment in Scala:

WorkingWithScriptsAndClasses/UseInvestment.scala

```
import investments._

object UseInvestment {
  def main(args: Array[String]) {
    val investment = new Investment("XYZ Corporation", InvestmentType.STOCK)
    println(investment.getClass())
  }
}
```

If the bytecode compiled from the previous Java files is located in a directory named classes/investments, we can use it to compile our Scala file as follows:

```
scalac -classpath classes UseInvestment.scala
```

Once we compile, we can run our code like this:

```
scala -classpath classes:. UseInvestment
```

Alternately, we can also run it using the java tool:

```
java -classpath \
/opt/scala/scala-2.7.4.final/lib/scala-library.jar:classes:. UseInvestment
```

The output looks like this:

```
class investments.Investment
```

You have to use caution with the yield() method of the Investment class. If your Java code has methods or field names (like trait, yield, and so on) that conflict with Scala keywords, the Scala compiler will choke up when you call them. For example, the following code will not work:

```
val theYield1 = investment.yield   //ERROR
val theYield2 = investment.yield() //ERROR
```

Fortunately, Scala offers a solution. You can place the offending variables/methods in a backtick to get around the problem. So, we can get the previous two calls to work by modifying the code as follows:

```
val theYield1 = investment.`yield`
val theYield2 = investment.`yield`()
```

11.3 Using Scala Classes in Java

Scala provides full round-trip interoperability with Java. Since Scala compiles to bytecode, you can use Scala classes in Java quite easily. Remember, Scala does not by default follow the JavaBean convention, and you'll have to use the @scala.reflect.BeanProperty annotation to generate JavaBean convention getters and setters (Section 4.2, *Defining Fields, Methods, and Constructors*, on page 46). You can also inherit your Java classes from Scala classes. However, to run your Java code that uses Scala classes, you'll need scala-library.jar in your classpath. In this section, let's look at how different constructs in Scala manifest on the Java side.

Scala Classes with Normal and Higher-Order Functions

Scala classes that follow standard Java constructs are pretty straightforward, and you can use them readily on the Java side. Let's write a Scala class:

WorkingWithScriptsAndClasses/Car.scala

```
package automobiles

class Car(val year: Int) {
  private[this] var miles : Int = 0

  def drive(distance: Int) { miles += distance }

  override def toString() : String = "year: " + year + " miles: " + miles
}
```

Here's a sample Java class that uses this Scala class:

WorkingWithScriptsAndClasses/UseCar.java

```
//Java code

package automobiles.users;
import automobiles.Car;

public class UseCar {
  public static void main(String[] args) {
    Car car = new Car(2009);

    System.out.println(car);
    car.drive(10);
    System.out.println(car);
  }
}
```

We'll have to compile the Scala code using scalac and the Java code using javac:

```
scalac -d classes Car.scala
javac -d classes -classpath classes UseCar.java
java -classpath \
/opt/scala/scala-2.7.4.final/lib/scala-library.jar:classes automobiles.users.UseCar
```

In the previous example, we have placed the generated bytecode in the classes directory. That was pretty simple to use the Scala class in Java. However, not all Scala classes will be that kind to you. For instance, if your Scala classes have methods that accept closures, those methods are not usable in Java since Java does not currently support closures. The simulate() method in the Equipment class shown here is not usable from Java; however, we can use the run() method:

WorkingWithScriptsAndClasses/Equipment.scala

```
class Equipment {
  // Not usable from Java
  def simulate(input: Int)(calculator: Int => Int) : Int = {
    //...
    calculator(input)
  }

  def run(duration: Int) {
   println("running")
   //...
  }
}
```

So, when designing your API, if your class will primarily be used from Java, provide normal methods in addition to higher-order methods for your class to be fully usable from Java.

Working with Traits

Let's understand the restrictions for using traits with Java. Traits with no method implementation are simple interfaces at the bytecode level. Scala does not support the interface keyword. So, if you want to create interfaces in Scala, create traits with no implementation in them. Here is an example of a Scala trait, which is also an interface:

WorkingWithScriptsAndClasses/Writable.scala

```
trait Writable {
  def write(message: String) : Unit
}
```

The previous trait has one abstract method that should be implemented by any class that mixes in this trait. On the Java side, Writable is seen like any other interface; it has no dependency on Scala at all. So, we can implement it like this:

WorkingWithScriptsAndClasses/AWritableJavaClass.java

```java
//Java code
public class AWritableJavaClass implements Writable {
  public void write(String message) {}
}
```

However, if a trait has method implementations, then Java classes can't implement that trait/interface, though they can use it. So, while we can't implement Printable in Java, we can hold a reference to a Printable on the Java side:

WorkingWithScriptsAndClasses/Printable.scala

```scala
trait Printable {
  def print() {} // default print nothing
}
```

If you intend for your Java classes to implement a trait, then make it pure; in other words, have no implementation in it. Any common implementation in this case should go into an abstract base class instead of a trait. However, if you intend for Java classes to use a trait only, then you have no restrictions.

Singleton Objects and Companion Objects

Scala compiles the objects (singleton or companion) into a "singleton class"—a class with a special $ symbol at the end of its name. So, object Single, shown next, will result in a class named Single$. Scala, however, treats a singleton and a companion object differently, as you'll soon see.

Scala compiles a singleton object into a singleton class (using Java static methods). In addition, it also creates a regular class with methods that forward calls to the singleton class. So, for example, this code defines a singleton object Single, and Scala creates two classes, Single$ and the forward class Single:

WorkingWithScriptsAndClasses/Single.scala

```scala
object Single {
  def greet() { println("Hello from Single") }
}
```

We can use the previous singleton object in Java as we'd use a Java class with static methods, as shown here:

WorkingWithScriptsAndClasses/SingleUser.java

```java
//Java code
public class SingleUser {
  public static void main(String[] args) {
    Single.greet();
  }
}
```

The output from the previous code is shown here:

```
Hello from Single
```

If your object is a companion object to a class with the same name, Scala creates two classes, one for the class (Buddy in the following example) that represents the Scala class and the other for the companion object (Buddy$ in the following example):

WorkingWithScriptsAndClasses/Buddy.scala

```scala
class Buddy {
  def greet() { println("Hello from Buddy class") }
}

object Buddy {
  def greet() { println("Hello from Buddy object") }
}
```

To access the companion class, use the name of the class directly. To use its companion object, however, you need to use a special symbol MODULE$, as in this example:

WorkingWithScriptsAndClasses/BuddyUser.java

```java
//Java code
public class BuddyUser {
  public static void main(String[] args) {
    new Buddy().greet();
    Buddy$.MODULE$.greet();
  }
}
```

Here's the output:

```
Hello from Buddy class
Hello from Buddy object
```

11.4 Extending Classes

You can extend a Java class from a Scala class, and vice versa. For the most part, this should just work. As discussed earlier, if your methods accept closures as parameters, you will have trouble overriding them. Exceptions are also a problem.

Scala does not have the throws clause. In Scala you can throw any exception from any method without having to explicitly declare that as part of the method signature. However, if you override such a method in Java, you'll run into trouble when you try to throw an exception. Let's look at an example. Suppose we have a Bird defined in Scala:

```
abstract class Bird {
 def fly();
 //...
}
```

We also have another class Ostrich:

WorkingWithScriptsAndClasses/Ostrich.scala

```
class Ostrich extends Bird {
  def fly() {
    throw new NoFlyException
  }
  //...
}
```

where NoFlyException is defined like this:

WorkingWithScriptsAndClasses/NoFlyException.scala

```
class NoFlyException extends Exception {}
```

In the previous code, Ostrich's fly() method was able to throw the exception without any problem. However, if we implement a nonflying bird in Java, we'll run into trouble, as shown here:

WorkingWithScriptsAndClasses/Penguin.java

```
//Java code
class Penguin extends Bird {
  public void fly() throws NoFlyException {
    throw new NoFlyException();
  }
  //...
}
```

First, if we simply throw the exception, Java will complain "unreported exception NoFlyException; must be caught or declared to be thrown."

Once we add the throws clause, Java will complain "fly() in Penguin can-not override fly() in Bird; overridden method does not throw NoFlyEx-ception."

Even though Scala is flexible and does not insist that you specify what exceptions you throw, if you intend to extend from those methods in Java, you'll have to ask the Scala compiler to emit those details in the method signature. Scala provides a backdoor for that by defining the @throws annotation.

Even though Scala supports annotations, it does not provide any syn-tax to create an annotation. If you'd like to create your own annotations, you'll have to do that using Java. @throws is an annotation already pro-vided for you to express the checked exceptions your methods throw. So, for us to implement the Penguin in Java, we have to modify Bird like this:

WorkingWithScriptsAndClasses/Bird.scala

```scala
abstract class Bird {
 @throws(classOf[NoFlyException]) def fly();
  //...
}
```

Now when we compile the previous class, the Scala compiler will place the necessary signature for the fly() method in the bytecode. Your Pen-guin Java class will compile with no errors after this change.

You saw how easy it is to intermix Java and Scala. For constructs that are identical, it feels like you're simply using other Java classes. You learned how to work with constructs that are supported in one lan-guage, but not in the other. One of the key strengths of Scala is that it supports the Java semantics and extends it further with functional style. When working with enterprise applications and legacy code, you don't have to throw away your investments. You can easily intermix Scala with your existing Java code in your applications.

Chapter 12

Unit Testing with Scala

Your code always does what you type—unit testing helps you to assert that your code does what you meant. As you evolve your application, unit testing further helps ensure your code continues to meet those expectations.

Learning to write unit tests in Scala will benefit you in a number of ways:

- It is a nice way to introduce Scala on your current projects. Even though your production code is in Java, you can write the test code in Scala.
- It is a good way to learn Scala itself. As you learn the language, you can experiment with the language and its API by writing test cases.
- It improves your design. It is very hard to unit test code that is large and complex. In order to test it, you'd end up making the code smaller. This will lead to a better design by making the code more cohesive, loosely coupled, easier to understand, and easier to maintain.

Unit testing is a low-hanging fruit in Scala. You have three options— you can use JUnit, TestNG, or ScalaTest. We will start with JUnit in this chapter and then see how to use ScalaTest, which is a tool written in Scala.

12.1 Using JUnit

Using JUnit to run tests written in Scala is really simple. Since Scala compiles to Java bytecode, you can write your tests in Scala, use scalac to compile your code into bytecode, and then run your tests like you normally run JUnit test cases. You simply need to remember to include the Scala library in your classpath. Let's look at an example of writing a JUnit test in Scala:

UnitTestingWithScala/SampleTest.scala

```scala
import java.util.ArrayList
import org.junit.Test
import org.junit.Assert._

class SampleTest {
  @Test def listAdd() {
    val list = new ArrayList[String]
    list.add("Milk")
    list add "Sugar"

    assertEquals(2, list.size())
  }
}
```

In the previous code we imported java.util.AraryList and then org.junit.Test. We also included all the methods of org.junit.Assert. This serves as a static import popularized in Java 5. Our test class, SampleTest, has one test method, listAdd(), decorated by the JUnit 4.0 Test annotation. Within the test method, we created an instance of ArrayList and first added the String "Milk" to it. That is pure Java syntax without the semicolon at the end. On the other hand, the next addition of "Sugar" illustrates some syntax sugar in Scala—it allowed us to drop the . and the parentheses. You can enjoy such lightweight syntax when writing your unit tests in Scala. Finally, we assert that the ArrayList instance has two elements in it.

We can compile this code using scalac and run this code like we'd typically run any JUnit test. Here are the commands to do that:

```
scalac -classpath $JUNITJAR:. SampleTest.scala
java -classpath $SCALALIBRARY:$JUNITJAR:. org.junit.runner.JUnitCore SampleTest
```

I have set $JUNITJAR and $SCALALIBRARY environmental variables on my machine to the location of the JUnit JAR and Scala library JAR, respectively. Here's the result of the command to execute the test:

```
JUnit version 4.5
.
Time: 0.02

OK (1 test)
```

See how simple it is to write a JUnit test in Scala? You benefit further by taking advantage of familiar Scala idioms to clarify your code. So, it is pretty straightforward to use JUnit or TestNG in Scala to test Java code, Scala code, or any code written for the Java platform, for that matter. Next we'll see what advantage ScalaTest provides over using JUnit.

12.2   Using ScalaTest

JUnit and TestNG are both good starting points for unit testing Scala code. However, as you get more familiar with Scala, you'll want to take advantage of Scala's conciseness and idioms for unit testing as well. When you're ready for that, you may want to graduate to using ScalaT-est. ScalaTest is a testing framework written in Scala by Bill Venners et al. It provides concise syntax for assertions and functional style for testing both Scala and Java code.

ScalaTest does not ship with Scala, so first you need to download it from http://www.artima.com/scalatest. Once you download scalatest-0.9.5.zip, unzip it near the location where you installed Scala. On my Mac OS X machine, I have it in the /opt/scala directory. On my Windows machine, it is under the C:\programs\scala directory.

12.3   Start with a Canary Test

Let's start with a canary test,[1] which is a very simple test to make sure the framework is installed on your system and you are able to use it properly:

UnitTestingWithScala/CanaryTest.scala
```
class CanaryTest extends org.scalatest.Suite {
  def testOK() {
    assert(true)
  }
}

(new CanaryTest).execute()
```

We extended CanaryTest from the class Suite that's part of ScalaTest. We wrote a test method testOK() that asserted true is actually true—very basic to make sure things work. To run this test, we instantiate an

---

1. http://memeagora.blogspot.com/2007/06/coalmine-canary-tests.html

instance of our suite and call the execute() method on it. To run this test, type the following:

```
scala -classpath $SCALATEST:. CanaryTest.scala
```

Set the classpath accordingly based on the system you are on. Here's the output:

```
Test Starting - Main$$anon$1$CanaryTest.testOK
Test Succeeded - Main$$anon$1$CanaryTest.testOK
```

It reported the names of the test(s) it ran. It did not complain—the test ran successfully. If the test had failed, we would've gotten a long message. The previous test suite contained only one test. However, you certainly may have more than one test per test suite.

12.4 Using Runner

If you want to execute more than one test suite, you can use the Runner class provided in ScalaTest.[2] It allows you to selectively include and exclude test suites, as well as to attach different kind of reporters to display the result of running tests. For a full description of various options, refer to the documentation provided for ScalaTest (see Appendix A, on page 207).

Let's look at an example of using Runner. Suppose we have a test suite named ListTest:

> UnitTestingWithScala/ListTest.scala

```
class ListTest extends org.scalatest.Suite {
  def testListEmpty() {
    val list = new java.util.ArrayList[Integer]
    assert(0 == list.size)
  }

  def testListAdd() {
    val list = new java.util.ArrayList[Integer]
    list.add(1)
    list add 4
    assert(2 == list.size)
  }
}
```

---

2. ScalaTest also provides a SuperSuite that you can extend and use to nest other suites. However, Runner requires no coding and provides autodiscovery of suites.

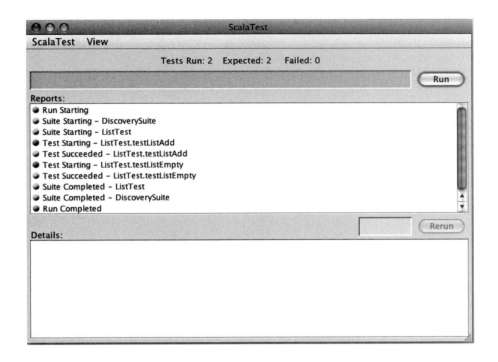

Figure 12.1: USING RUNNER TO EXECUTE SCALATEST

We can compile and run it using the following commands:

```
scalac -classpath $SCALATEST ListTest.scala
```

```
scala -classpath $SCALATEST:. org.scalatest.tools.Runner -p .
```

The -p option specifies the directories where Runner will look for test suites. Since we did not specify any particular test suite, it will pick up all compiled test suites in the given path. The output from the previous code is shown in Figure 12.1. If you don't see all the details about each of the tests, you can play with the items in the View menu.

If you are a command-line type (like your humble author), you can use the -o option to direct the test execution results to standard output instead of a GUI. Here is how to achieve that:

```
scalac -classpath $SCALATEST ListTest.scala
```

```
scala -classpath $SCALATEST:. org.scalatest.tools.Runner -p . -o
```

Here's the result:

```
Run starting. Expected test count is: 2
Suite Starting - DiscoverySuite: The execute method of a nested suite is
  about to be invoked.
Suite Starting - ListTest: The execute method of a nested suite is about
  to be invoked.
Test Starting - ListTest.testListAdd
Test Succeeded - ListTest.testListAdd
Test Starting - ListTest.testListEmpty
Test Succeeded - ListTest.testListEmpty
Suite Completed - ListTest: The execute method of a nested suite returned
  normally.
Suite Completed - DiscoverySuite: The execute method of a nested suite
  returned normally.
Run completed. Total number of tests run was: 2
All tests passed.
```

Alternately, you can also use an -f option to redirect to a file. This can be very useful for logging results and processing them during continuous integration.[3]

12.5 Asserts

ScalaTest provides a simple assert() method.[4] It checks whether the expression in the parameter evaluates to true.[5] If the expression evaluates to true, the assert() method returns silently. Otherwise, it throws an AssertionError. Here is an example of assertion failure:

UnitTestingWithScala/AssertionFailureExample.scala

```scala
class AssertionFailureExample extends org.scalatest.Suite {
  def testAssertFailure() {
    assert(2 == List().size)
  }
}

(new AssertionFailureExample).execute()
```

---

3. See "Continuous Integration" in Appendix A, on page 207, and Mike Clark's *Pragmatic Project Automation* [Cla04] and *Continuous Integration* [DMG07] by Duvall et al.
4. You can also import and use JUnit, TestNG, or Hamcrest matchers methods like assertEquals() and assertThat(). Be sure to include the appropriate JAR files.
5. A variation of assert() checks whether the parameter evaluates to None.

When we run the previous test, we get an error message that includes the following information:

```
Test Starting - Main$$anon$1$AssertionFailureExample.testAssertFailure
TEST FAILED - Main$$anon$1$AssertionFailureExample.testAssertFailure
  ((virtual file):7)
org.scalatest.TestFailedException:
...
```

The test indicated a failure, but the message is not very helpful. If you have a number of tests, you'd like to get more information than mere "something failed." ScalaTest provides the convenient operator === that prints some more details than the assert() method. Here is an example using this feature:

UnitTestingWithScala/AssertionFailureExample2.scala
```
class AssertionFailureExample2 extends org.scalatest.Suite {
  def testAssertFailure() {
    assert(2 === List().size)
  }
}

(new AssertionFailureExample2).execute()
```

When we run the previous test, we will get an error message that includes the following information:

```
Test Starting - Main$$anon$1$AssertionFailureExample2.testAssertFailure
TEST FAILED - Main$$anon$1$AssertionFailureExample2.testAssertFailure:
  2 did not equal 0 ((virtual file):7)
org.scalatest.TestFailedException: 2 did not equal 0
...
```

From the output you can gather that 2 is not equal to 0. That certainly is more helpful than what assert() told us previously. However, the message lacks context, and it would be nice to have some more details on what these numbers actually mean. Thankfully, assert() allows you to send an additional parameter with a meaningful message:

UnitTestingWithScala/AssertionFailureWithMessage.scala
```
class AssertionFailureWithMessage extends org.scalatest.Suite {
  def testAssertFailure() {
    assert(2 === List().size, "Unexpected size of List")
  }
}

(new AssertionFailureWithMessage).execute()
```

When we run the previous test, we get more meaningful information:

```
Test Starting - Main$$anon$1$AssertionFailureWithMessage.testAssertFailure
TEST FAILED - Main$$anon$1$AssertionFailureWithMessage.testAssertFailure:
  Unexpected size of List
2 did not equal 0 ((virtual file):7)
org.scalatest.TestFailedException: Unexpected size of List
2 did not equal 0
...
```

If you're checking for the equality of values (like the JUnit assertEquals() method), you will like the expect() method of ScalaTest:

UnitTestingWithScala/ExpectExample.scala

```
class ExpectExample extends org.scalatest.Suite {
  def testAssertFailure() {
    expect(2, "Unexpected List size") { List().size }
    // The above exception is wrong
  }
}

(new ExpectExample).execute()
```

Here's the output:

```
Test Starting - Main$$anon$1$ExpectExample.testAssertFailure
TEST FAILED - Main$$anon$1$ExpectExample.testAssertFailure:
  Unexpected List size
Expected 2, but got 0 ((virtual file):7)
org.scalatest.TestFailedException: Unexpected List size
Expected 2, but got 0
...
```

The expect() method accepts the expected value, an optional message, and a closure. The closure holds the expression to be evaluated, and the expect() method ensures that the expression evaluated to the given expected value. Otherwise, it throws an AssertionError.

The expect() method is fairly concise, is readable, and provides the right level of message on failure. So, I prefer this method over assert() for comparing values.

12.6 Exception Tests

Exception tests are useful to ensure that the unit of code under test is throwing the expected exceptions.

Here is an example of an exception test:

```scala
def testGetOnEmptyList() {
  try {
    val list = new java.util.ArrayList[Integer]
    list.get(0)
    fail("Expected exception for getting element from empty list")
  }
  catch {
    case ex: IndexOutOfBoundsException => // :) Success
  }
}
```

When we create an instance of java.util.ArrayList, the list is empty. Now, in the test, we try to get hold of the missing first element and expect an IndexOutOfBoundsException exception to be thrown. If the get() method throws that exception or its subclass, the catch[6] will handle it, indicating the code behaved as expected. If the method throws some other exception, it will go unhandled, and the test will fail. Also, if the method did not throw any exception, the test will fail executing the fail() method. I call this the land-mine method, because it blows up if we step on it.

The previous exception test does its job, but it's verbose. Furthermore, it will not tell you if you forgot to call the fail() method. You'd expect this to be concise,[7] and ScalaTest's intercept() method will stand up to that expectation. The previous verbose test can be written concisely using intercept():

```scala
def testGetOnEmptyList_Concise() {
    val list = new java.util.ArrayList[Integer]
    intercept(classOf[IndexOutOfBoundsException],
        "Expected exception for getting element from empty list") {
      list.get(0)
    }

    //You'll get a deprecation warning from the statement above.
    //ScalaTest is evolving to use a newer style for intercept.
    //Currently the new style does not take an error message argument.
    //When it does, you should use
    //intercept[IndexOutOfBoundsException] ("Expected ...") {...}
}
```

The intercept() method takes the expected exception class as a parameter, an optional error message, and a closure containing the expression

---

6. Scala's try-catch-finally semantics are the same as Java's. However, its catch syntax is different—it uses pattern matching syntax (see Chapter 9, *Pattern Matching and Regular Expressions*, on page 109).

7. See my blog "Prefer Conciseness over Terseness" at http://tinyurl.com/5bawat.

that is expected to throw the given exception. If the expected exception or its subclass is thrown by the expression, the intercept() method catches that exception and returns it to us—we can use this result, if we desire, to check further for a specific exception message. If the expression did not throw any exception or threw another unexpected exception, the intercept() method will fail.

12.7 Sharing Code Between Tests

If you have common code you'd like to share between tests, there are two options available in ScalaTest. Assume we want to write multiple tests for the java.util.ArrayList class. Instead of creating an instance in each method, it would be good to create it in a common method—that will make the code DRY.[8] Let's explore the two options—the first one is similar to what JUnit offers, and the second one takes advantage of closures.

Sharing Code Using BeforeAndAfter

You can mix in ScalaTest's BeforeAndAfter trait into your test suite—this provides a beforeEach() method and an afterEach() method. These two are similar to setUp() and tearDown() of JUnit, respectively, and sandwich each of the test methods—beforeEach() automatically runs before each test, and afterEach() runs automatically after. BeforeAndAfter also provides a beforeAll() that executes once before any test in that suite is executed and provides an afterAll() that runs once, at the end, after all tests have executed. Let's look at an example of using beforeEach() and afterEach():

UnitTestingWithScala/ShareCodeImperative.scala

```
class ShareCodeImperative extends org.scalatest.Suite
  with org.scalatest.BeforeAndAfter {
  var list : java.util.ArrayList[Integer] = _

  override def beforeEach() { list = new java.util.ArrayList[Integer] }

  override def afterEach() { list = null }

  def testListEmptyOnCreate() {
    expect(0, "Expected size to be 0") { list.size() }
  }
```

---

8. See "Don't Repeat Yourself" in *The Pragmatic Programmer* [HT00].

```
    def testGetOnEmptyList() {
      intercept[IndexOutOfBoundsException] { list.get(0) }
    }
  }
}

(new ShareCodeImperative).execute()
```

Our ShareCodeImperative mixes in BeforeAndAfter and overrides the
beforeEach() and afterEach() methods. Within the beforeEach() method,
we instantiate an instance of java.util.ArrayList and store it in the field list
of ShareCodeImperative. Each test now uses instances of ArrayList freshly
created right before they're executed. Once the tests complete, the
afterEach() method sets the reference to null—this operation is redundant, but in general, if you have any meaningful cleanup to do, this is
the place.

Sharing Code Using Closures

In the previous example, we had to create a field list in the test suite,
and we assigned to it repeatedly in each invocation of the beforeEach()
method. That is imperative style—we risk having some fields in our
class that may be passed between tests. One of the tenets of unit testing is that the tests must be isolated from each other. You can ensure
isolation by properly writing the beforeEach() and afterEach() methods.
Alternately, you can completely avoid the fields, and the associated
problems, using more of a functional style using closures, as we'll see
next. Here is an example:

UnitTestingWithScala/ShareCodeFunctional.scala

```
class ShareCodeFunctional extends org.scalatest.Suite {
  def withList(testFunction : (java.util.ArrayList[Integer]) => Unit) {
    val list = new java.util.ArrayList[Integer]

    try {
      testFunction(list)
    }
    finally {
      // perform any necessary cleanup here after return
    }
  }

  def testListEmptyOnCreate() {
    withList { list => expect(0, "Expected size to be 0") { list.size() } }
  }
```

```
    def testGetOnEmptyList() {
      withList {
        list => intercept[IndexOutOfBoundsException] { list.get(0) }
      }
    }
}

(new ShareCodeFunctional).execute()
```

Our class ShareCodeFunctional extends the now familiar Suite. The method withList() accepts a closure as a parameter—that stuff within the parentheses of the method declaration defines the signature of a closure it expects. The signature declares a closure that takes an ArrayList and returns Unit (the void type in Scala). testFunction is the name we've given to the closure parameter of withList().

Within the withList() method, we create an instance of ArrayList and assign it to a local constant named list—this was declared as a var in the Before-AndAfter example. We then invoke the given closure, testFunction, with the list as an argument. Upon return from the test method, we can perform any necessary cleanup. That's another example of the use of the Execute Around Method pattern (see Section 6.7, *Execute Around Method Pattern*, on page 76).

Within each of the test methods, we call withList() and present it with a closure that performs the actual test using the list created by withList(). We can create more of these initialization methods like withList() and use them in other tests. So, we can pick and choose between different initialization and cleanup pairs. This makes the initialization and cleanup we use much more visible and clearer to the reader of the test. In turn, that will make it easier to follow what's going on in each test.

12.8 Functional Style with FunSuite

ScalaTest provides a FunSuite that allows you to write your tests in a functional style with more flexibility to name your tests. Instead of writing test methods, you invoke a method named test() and pass it a descriptive name for the test and a closure that contains the body of the test. Let's rewrite the code in Section 12.7, *Sharing Code Using Closures*, on the preceding page using FunSuite.

UnitTestingWithScala/UsingFunSuite.scala

```
class UsingFunSuite extends org.scalatest.FunSuite {
  def withList(testFunction : (java.util.ArrayList[Integer]) => Unit) {
    val list = new java.util.ArrayList[Integer]

    try {
      testFunction(list)
    }
    finally {
      // perform any necessary cleanup here after return
    }
  }

  test("Check if the list is Empty On Creation") {
    withList { list => expect(0, "Expected size to be 0") { list.size() } }
  }

  test("Get must throw exception when called on an empty list") {
    withList {
      list => intercept[IndexOutOfBoundsException] { list.get(0) }
    }
  }
}

(new UsingFunSuite).execute()
```

Here are the results:

```
Test Starting - Main$$anon$1$UsingFunSuite: Check if the list is Empty
  On Creation
Test Succeeded - Main$$anon$1$UsingFunSuite: Check if the list is Empty
  On Creation
Test Starting - Main$$anon$1$UsingFunSuite: Get must throw exception
  when called on an empty list
Test Succeeded - Main$$anon$1$UsingFunSuite: Get must throw exception
  when called on an empty list
```

Instead of the traditional test methods, we invoked FunSuite's test() method and provided descriptive messages. The actual test code is nicely nested in the closures attached to each call to the test() method. You will find this form of test is fairly lightweight compared to the traditional tests you write, and it may soon become your favorite way to express tests in Scala.

12.9 Running ScalaTests Using JUnit

OK, you have now fallen in love with ScalaTest but quickly realize that most of your current tests in your projects are in JUnit (or TestNG).

You wonder whether you can take advantage of the concise syntax and features of ScalaTest and still run your tests using JUnit (or TestNG). JUnit3Suite for JUnit (or TestNGSuite for TestNG) allows you to do just that. You simply extend your test suite from JUnit3Suite and write your test methods like you would for JUnit to recognize. Within the test methods, you can make use of ScalaTest's assert(), expect(), and intercept() and of the functional style of sharing code we discussed earlier. You can run your tests now using either ScalaTest or JUnit. This supports only JUnit 3.*x* style (tested with JUnit 3.8.1) and not the JUnit 4.0 style. Here is an example using JUnit3Suite:

UnitTestingWithScala/UsingJUnit3Suite.scala

```scala
class UsingJUnit3Suite extends org.scalatest.junit.JUnit3Suite {
  def withList(testFunction : (java.util.ArrayList[Integer]) => Unit) {
    val list = new java.util.ArrayList[Integer]

    try {
      testFuntcion(list)
    }
    finally {
      // perform any necessary cleanup here after return
    }
  }

  def testListEmptyOnCreate() {
    withList { list => expect(0, "Expected size to be 0") { list.size() } }
  }

  def testGetOnEmptyList() {
    withList {
      list => intercept[IndexOutOfBoundsException] { list.get(0) }
    }
  }
}
```

Here is some sample Scala code to run the previous test using JUnit:

UnitTestingWithScala/RunJUnitTest.scala

```scala
object RunJUnitTest {
  def main(args: Array[String]) =
    junit.textui.TestRunner.run(classOf[UsingJUnit3Suite])
}
```

We can compile and run the previous code using ScalaTest or JUnit.

The following example shows you how to compile and run it using both tools:

```
scalac -classpath $SCALATEST:$JUNITJAR:. \
  UsingJUnit3Suite.scala RunJUnitTest.scala
echo "Running ScalaTest"
scala -classpath $SCALATEST:$JUNITJAR:. \
  org.scalatest.tools.Runner -o -p . -s UsingJUnit3Suite
echo "Running JUNIT test"
java -classpath $SCALALIBRARY:$SCALATEST:$JUNITJAR:. RunJUnitTest
```

The output from the previous example is shown here:

```
Running ScalaTest
Run starting. Expected test count is: 2
Suite Starting - UsingJUnit3Suite: The execute method of a nested suite
  is about to be invoked.
Suite Starting - UsingJUnit3Suite: UsingJUnit3Suite
Test Starting - testGetOnEmptyList: UsingJUnit3Suite
Test Succeeded - testGetOnEmptyList: UsingJUnit3Suite
Test Starting - testListEmptyOnCreate: UsingJUnit3Suite
Test Succeeded - testListEmptyOnCreate: UsingJUnit3Suite
Suite Completed - UsingJUnit3Suite: UsingJUnit3Suite
Suite Completed - UsingJUnit3Suite: The execute method of a nested
  suite returned normally.
Run completed. Total number of tests run was: 2
All tests passed.
Running JUNIT test
..
Time: 0.02

OK (2 tests)
```

In the previous example, you saw how to run the test we wrote with ScalaTest using both Scala and JUnit. This features lowers the barrier of entry to introduce Scala for unit testing on current projects. You now don't have to chose between JUnit (or TestNG) and ScalaTest. You can mix them and take advantage of the conciseness offered by Scala and at the same time continue with the well-established frameworks on our projects.

When writing unit tests, you'll often rely on using mock objects to stub or mock the code that the code under test depends on. If you use frameworks like EasyMock or JMock to create mock objects, you can use them readily in Scala as well. While putting those frameworks for mocking to use, you can take advantage of Scala features such as traits, functional style, and conciseness.

You're now equipped with very important tools and practices in this chapter. However, you probably know that unit testing requires more than these tools—it requires personal discipline and commitment. I hope the elegance of writing tests in Scala along with the facilities provided by ScalaTest serve as a catalyst in motivating you to write or continue to write your unit tests. In the next chapter, we will explore how exception handling is similar and different from Java.

Chapter 13

Exception Handling

Java's checked exceptions force you to catch exceptions you don't care to handle. That often leads to programmers placing empty catch blocks, thus suppressing exceptions instead of naturally propagating them to be handled at the right place. Scala does not do that. It lets you handle exceptions you care about and leave out the rest. What you don't handle is propagated up automatically. In this chapter, you'll learn how to handle exceptions in Scala.

13.1 Exception Handling

Scala supports the Java semantics for exception handling, but it does so with a different syntax. In Scala you throw exceptions just like you do in Java:[1]

```
throw new WhatEverException
```

Also, you place a try just like in Java. Scala, however, does not force you to catch exceptions that you don't care about—not even checked exceptions. This prevents you from adding unnecessary catch blocks in your code—you simply let the exceptions you don't care to catch propagate up the chain. So, if we want to call the Thread's sleep(), for example, instead of this:

```
// Java code
try {
  Thread.sleep(1000);
}
catch(InterruptedException ex) {
  // Losing sleep over what to do here?
}
```

---

1. You can leave out the empty parentheses when you instantiate.

we can simply write this:

```
Thread.sleep(1000)
```

So, Scala did not insist that we write an unnecessary try-catch block.

Of course, you certainly should handle exceptions you can do something about—that's what catch is for. The syntax of catch is quite different in Scala; you use pattern matching for handling the exceptions. Let's look at an example:

ScalaForTheJavaEyes/ExceptionHandling.scala

```
def taxFor(amount: Double) : String = {
  if (amount < 0)
    throw new IllegalArgumentException("Amount must be greater than zero")
  if (amount < 0.1) throw new RuntimeException("Amount too small to be taxed")
  if (amount > 1000000) throw new Exception("Amount too large...")
  "Tax for $" + amount + " is $"+ amount * 0.08
}

for (amount <- List(100.0, 0.09, -2.0, 1000001.0)) {
  try {
    println(taxFor(amount))
  }
  catch {
    case ex: IllegalArgumentException => println(ex.getMessage())
    case ex: RuntimeException => {
      // if you need a block of code to handle exception
      println("Don't bother reporting..." + ex.getMessage())
    }
  }
}
```

The output from the previous code (with a partial stack trace) is shown here:

```
Tax for $100.0 is $8.0
Don't bother reporting...Amount too small to be taxed
Amount must be greater than zero
java.lang.Exception: Amount too large...
        at Main$$anon$1.taxFor((virtual file):9)
        at Main$$anon$1$$anonfun$1.apply((virtual file):15)
        at Main$$anon$1$$anonfun$1.apply((virtual file):13)
        at scala.List.foreach(List.scala:841)
        at Main$$anon$1.<init>((virtual file):13)
        at Main$.main((virtual file):4)
...
```

The taxFor() method throws three different exceptions depending on the input. The catch block has case statements for handling two of these exceptions. The previous output shows how these blocks handled these two exceptions. The third unhandled exception results in termination of the program with details of the stack trace being printed. The order of the case statements is important, as we discuss in Section 13.2, *Mind the Catch Order*, on the next page.

Scala also supports the finally block—just as in Java, it's executed irrespective of whether the code in the try block threw an exception.

In the previous example, we saw how to catch specific exceptions. If we want to catch all exceptions, we can use the _ (underscore) for the case condition, as shown in the following example:

`ScalaForTheJavaEyes/CatchAll.scala`

```scala
def taxFor(amount: Double) : String = {
  if (amount < 0)
    throw new IllegalArgumentException("Amount must be greater than zero")
  if (amount < 0.1) throw new RuntimeException("Amount too small to be taxed")
  if (amount > 1000000) throw new Exception("Amount too large...")
  "Tax for $" + amount + " is $"+ amount * 0.08
}

for (amount <- List(100.0, 0.09, -2.0, 1000001.0)) {
  try {
    println(taxFor(amount))
  }
  catch {
    case ex : IllegalArgumentException => println(ex.getMessage())
    case _ => println("Something went wrong")
  }
}
```

The output from the previous code is shown here. The catchall case caught all but the IllegalArgumentException, which had its own special catch block:

```
Tax for $100.0 is $8.0
Something went wrong
Amount must be greater than zero
Something went wrong
```

Just as catching checked exceptions is optional in Scala, so too is declaring checked exceptions optional. Scala doesn't require you to declare what exceptions you intend to throw. See Section 11.4, *Extending Classes*, on page 160 for issues related to intermixing the code with Java.

13.2 Mind the Catch Order

When attempting to handle exceptions, Java watches over the order in which you place multiple catch blocks. The following example will give us a compilation error:

ScalaForTheJavaEyes/CatchOrder.java

```
//Java code---will not compile due to incorrect catch order

public class CatchOrder {
  public void catchOrderExample() {
    try {
      String str = "hello";
      System.out.println(str.charAt(31));
    }
    catch(Exception ex) { System.out.println("Exception caught"); }
    catch(StringIndexOutOfBoundsException ex) {
      System.out.println("Invalid Index"); }
  }
}
```

If we compile this code, we'll get the error message "exception java.lang. StringIndexOutOfBoundsException has already been caught." Scala uses pattern matching for its catch blocks (see Section 13.1, *Exception Handling*, on page 179), and that takes effect in the order in which you present. So, Scala does not warn you if a former statement handles exceptions that you intend to handle in later statements. Consider the following example:

ScalaForTheJavaEyes/CatchOrder.scala

```
try {
  val str = "hello"
  println(str(31))
}
catch {
  case ex : Exception => println("Exception caught")
  case ex : StringIndexOutOfBoundsException => println("Invalid Index")
}
```

The output from the previous code is shown here:

```
Exception caught
```

The first case matches Exception and all of its subclasses. When using multiple catch blocks, you must ensure that exceptions are being handled by the catch blocks you intend.

In this chapter, you saw how Scala provides a concise and elegant way to handle exceptions. Scala also does not require you to catch exceptions that you don't care to handle. This allows for the exception to be safely propagated to higher levels in code for proper handling.

Chapter 14

Using Scala

In this chapter, we'll bring together a lot of things you've learned so far in this book, and then some. We will progressively build an application that will allow us to find the net worth of our investments in the stock market. You'll see the benefit of Scala's conciseness and expressiveness, you'll learn the power of pattern matching along with function values/closures, and you will apply concurrency. In addition, you will also learn Scala's support for XML processing and how to build Swing applications.

14.1 The Net Asset Application

We'll build an application that takes a list of stock ticker symbols along with the units of stock users hold and tells them the total value of their investments as of the current date. This involves several things: getting users' input, reading files, parsing data, writing to files, fetching data from the Web, and displaying information to users.

We will first develop the application as a console application. Then we will convert it to a Swing application. Let's take one step at a time and refactor the application along the way. So, let's get started.

14.2 Getting Users' Input

As a first step, we want to know the ticker symbols and units of stock for which the application should find the values. Scala's Console class can help us get user input from the command line.

The following code helps us read this information into memory:

`UsingScala/ConsoleInput.scala`

```
print("Please enter a ticker symbol:")
val symbol = Console.readLine
//val symbol = readLine // This will work too
println("OK, got it, you own " + symbol)
```

A sample execution of the previous code is shown here:

```
scala ConsoleInput.scala
Please enter a ticker symbol:AAPL
OK, got it, you own AAPL
```

In the previous code, we invoked the readLine() method of the Scala Console singleton object. This object allows us to print to the terminal and also to read from the console. We can access the in property, which is an instance of java.io.BufferedReader, or call one of the many read convenience methods.

The println() method also belongs to this object. We have not prefixed the println() with Console so far in the examples we've seen. This is because the Predef object provides wrapper methods on select methods of Console. That is, Predef's printf() routes the call to Console's printf(). We could have dropped the Console. prefix to readLine() in the previous code if we wanted and could have used the method of Predef instead.

14.3 Reading and Writing Files

Now that we've figured how to get user input in Scala, it's time to see how to write data to a file. We can use the java.io.File object to achieve this. Here is an example of writing to a file:

`UsingScala/WriteToFile.scala`

```
import java.io._

val writer = new PrintWriter(new File("symbols.txt"))

writer write "AAPL"
writer.close()
```

The previous simple code writes the symbol "AAPL" to the file named symbols.txt. The content of the file is shown here:

`UsingScala/symbols.txt`

```
AAPL
```

Reading files is really simple. Scala's Source class and its companion object come in handy for this purpose. For illustration purposes, let's write a Scala script that reads itself:

UsingScala/ReadingFile.scala

```
import scala.io.Source

println("*** The content of the file you read is:")
Source.fromFile("ReadingFile.scala").foreach { print }

//to get each line call getLines() on Source instance
```

In the previous code, we read the file that contains this code and printed out its contents. (As you know, reading a file is not such a simple task in Java.) The output from the previous code is shown here:

```
*** The content of the file you read is:
import scala.io.Source

println("*** The content of the file you read is:")
Source.fromFile("ReadingFile.scala").foreach { print }

//to get each line call getLines() on Source instance
```

The Source class is an Iterator over the input stream. The Source companion object has several convenience methods to read from a file, an input stream, a string, or even a URL, as you'll see soon. The foreach() method helps you get one character at a time (the input is buffered, so no worries about performance). If you're interested in reading a line at a time, you'd use the getLines() method instead.

Very soon we will need to read information off the Web. So, while discussing Source, let's take a look at its fromURL() method. This method allows us to read the content of a website, a web service, or just about anything that we can point at using a URL. Here is an example that reads the Scala documentation site and determines the version number of Scala the document relates to:

UsingScala/ReadingURL.scala

```
import scala.io.Source
import java.net.URL

val source = Source.fromURL(
  new URL("http://www.scala-lang.org/docu/files/api/index.html"))

println(source.getLine(3))
val content = source.mkString
val VersionRegEx = """[\D\S]+scaladoc\s+\(version\s+(.+)\)[\D\S]+""".r
```

```
content match {
  case VersionRegEx(version) => println("Scala doc for version: " + version)
}
```

The output from the previous code is shown here:

```
        <head><title>Scala Library</title>
Scala doc for version: 2.7.4.final
```

In the previous code we called fromURL() to obtain a Source instance that will allow us to iterate over the content read from that URL. We then passed in 3 to the getLine() method to read the third line. You must use caution with this method. The index value starts with a 1 and not a 0, so the first line is actually referred to using the index 1.

We want to extract the version number from the content we received. We first called mkString() on the source instance. This gives us a string form of the entire content; that is, this method concatenated all the lines in the content. We then defined a regular expression to match and extract[1] the version details from the content. Finally, we used the match() method to extract the version details using pattern matching.

Although the previous example may quench your thirst to read and write files and access a URL, we need to get back to the net asset application. One approach is to store the ticker symbols and units as plain text. Reading the file is easy, but then parsing through the contents of the file to get various ticker symbols and units is not going to be that easy. As much as we all hate XML for its verbosity, it does come in handy to organize this kind of information and parse it. So, let's make use of it for the net asset application.

14.4 XML as a First-Class Citizen

Scala treats XML as a first-class citizen. So, instead of embedding XML documents into strings, you can place them inline in your code like you'd place an int or Double value. Let's take a look at an example:

UsingScala/UseXML.scala

```
val xmlFragment =
<symbols>
  <symbol ticker="AAPL"><units>200</units></symbol>
  <symbol ticker="IBM"><units>215</units></symbol>
</symbols>
```

---

1. See Chapter 9, *Pattern Matching and Regular Expressions*, on page 109 for details about extractors and regular expressions.

```
println(xmlFragment)
println(xmlFragment.getClass())
```

We created a *val* named xmlFragment and directly assigned it to some sample XML content. Scala parsed the XML content and happily created an instance of scala.xml.Elem for us, as shown in the following output:

```
<symbols>
  <symbol ticker="AAPL"><units>200</units></symbol>
  <symbol ticker="IBM"><units>215</units></symbol>
</symbols>
class scala.xml.Elem
```

The Scala package scala.xml provides classes to help us read XML documents, parse them, create them, and store them. One of the main reasons I wanted you to look at XML is it's easier to parse. So, let's take a look how easy it is.

You probably have played with XPath, which provides a very powerful way to query into an XML document. Scala provides an XPath-like query ability with one minor difference. Instead of using forward slashes (/ and //) to query, Scala uses backward slashes (\ and \\) for methods that help parse and extract. This difference was necessary since Scala follows the Java tradition of using the two forward slashes for comments. So, let's see how we can parse this XML fragment on hand.

We first want to get the symbol elements. We can use the XPath-like query for this, as shown here:

`UsingScala/UseXML.scala`

```
var symbolNodes = xmlFragment \ "symbol"
println(symbolNodes.mkString("\n"))
println(symbolNodes.getClass())
```

The output from the previous code is shown here:

```
<symbol ticker="AAPL"><units>200</units></symbol>
<symbol ticker="IBM"><units>215</units></symbol>
class scala.xml.NodeSeq$$anon$2
```

We called the \() method on the XML element and asked it to look for all symbol elements. It retuned an instance of scala.xml.NodeSeq, which represents a collection of XML nodes.

The \() method looks only for elements that are direct descendants of the target element (the symbols element in this example). If we want to search through all the elements in the hierarchy starting from the target element, use the \\() method, as shown here. Also, we can use the text() method to get the text node within an element.

UsingScala/UseXML.scala

```
var unitsNodes = xmlFragment \\ "units"
println(unitsNodes.mkString("\n"))
println(unitsNodes.getClass())
println(unitsNodes(0).text)
```

The output from the previous code is shown here:

```
<units>200</units>
<units>215</units>
class scala.xml.NodeSeq$$anon$2
200
```

In the previous example, we use the text() method to get the text node. We can also use pattern matching to get the text value and other contents. If we want to navigate the structure of an XML document, the methods \() and \\() are useful. However, if we want to find matching content anywhere in the XML document at arbitrary locations, pattern matching will be more useful.

We saw the power of pattern matching in Chapter 9, *Pattern Matching and Regular Expressions*, on page 109. Scala extends that power to matching XML fragments as well, as shown here:

UsingScala/UseXML.scala

```
unitsNodes(0) match {
  case <units>{numberOfUnits}</units> => println("Units: " + numberOfUnits)
}
```

The output from the previous code is shown here:

```
Units: 200
```

We took the first units element and asked Scala to extract the text value 200. In the case statement we provided the match for the fragment we're interested in and a variable, numberOfUnits, as a placeholder for the text content of that element.

That helped us get the units for one symbol. There are two problems, however. The previous approach works only if the content matches exactly with the expression in the case; that is, the units element contains only one content item or one child element. If it contains a mixture of child elements and text contents, the previous match will fail. Furthermore, we want to get the units for all symbols, not just the first one. We can ask Scala to grab all contents (elements and text) using the _* symbol, as shown here:

```
UsingScala/UseXML.scala
```
```
println("Ticker\tUnits")
xmlFragment match {
  case <symbols>{symbolNodes @ _* }</symbols> =>
    for(symbolNode @ <symbol>{_*}</symbol> <- symbolNodes) {
      println("%-7s %s".format(
        symbolNode \ "@ticker", (symbolNode \ "units").text))
    }
}
```

The output from the previous code is shown here:

```
Ticker  Units
AAPL    200
IBM     215
```

That was quite some dense code. Let's take the time to understand it.

By using the symbol _*, we asked to read everything between the <symbols> and </symbols> into the placeholder variable symbolNodes. We saw an example using the @ symbol to place a variable name in Section 9.3, *Matching Tuples and Lists*, on page 111. The good news is it reads everything. The bad news is it reads everything including the text nodes that represent the blank spaces in the XML fragment (you're quite used to this problem if you've used XML DOM parsers). So, when looping through the symbolNodes, we iterate over only the symbol elements by pattern matching once more, this time in the parameter to the for() method. Remember, the first parameter you provide for the for() method is a pattern (see Section 8.5, *The for Expression*, on page 105). Finally, we perform an XPath query to get to the attribute ticker (recollect from XPath that you use an @ prefix to indicate the attribute query) and the text value in the units elements.

14.5 Reading and Writing XML

Once we get an XML document in memory, we know how to parse it. The next step is to figure out how to get an XML document loaded into our program and how to save a document in memory to a file. As an example, let's load an XML file that contains symbols and units, increase the units by 1, and store the updated content back into another XML file. Let's first tackle the step of loading the file.

Here is a sample file stocks.xml that we will load:

`UsingScala/stocks.xml`

```
<symbols>
  <symbol ticker="AAPL"><units>200</units></symbol>
  <symbol ticker="ADBE"><units>125</units></symbol>
  <symbol ticker="ALU"><units>150</units></symbol>
  <symbol ticker="AMD"><units>150</units></symbol>
  <symbol ticker="CSCO"><units>250</units></symbol>
  <symbol ticker="HPQ"><units>225</units></symbol>
  <symbol ticker="IBM"><units>215</units></symbol>
  <symbol ticker="INTC"><units>160</units></symbol>
  <symbol ticker="MSFT"><units>190</units></symbol>
  <symbol ticker="NSM"><units>200</units></symbol>
  <symbol ticker="ORCL"><units>200</units></symbol>
  <symbol ticker="SYMC"><units>230</units></symbol>
  <symbol ticker="TXN"><units>190</units></symbol>
  <symbol ticker="VRSN"><units>200</units></symbol>
  <symbol ticker="XRX"><units>240</units></symbol>
</symbols>
```

The load() method of the XML singleton object in the scala.xml package will help load the file, as shown here:

`UsingScala/ReadWriteXML.scala`

```
import scala.xml._

val stocksAndUnits = XML.load("stocks.xml")
println(stocksAndUnits.getClass())
println("Loaded file has " + (stocksAndUnits \\ "symbol").size +
    " symbol elements")
```

You can see from the output shown next that the load() returned to us an scala.xml.Elem instance. You can also see that the loaded file (stocks.xml) contains fifteen symbol elements.

```
class scala.xml.Elem
Loaded file has 15 symbol elements
```

You already know how to parse the content of this document and store the symbols and the corresponding units in a Map. Here's the code that does just that:

`UsingScala/ReadWriteXML.scala`

```
val stocksAndUnitsMap =
  (Map[String, Int]() /: (stocksAndUnits \ "symbol")) { (map, symbolNode) =>
    val ticker = (symbolNode \ "@ticker").toString
    val units = (symbolNode \ "units").text.toInt
    map(ticker) = units //Creates and returns a new Map
  }

println("Number of symbol elements found is " + stocksAndUnitsMap.size)
```

In the previous code, as we processed each symbol element, we accumulated the symbol and the corresponding units into a new Map. In the following output, you can see the number of symbols we loaded from the document:

```
Number of symbol elements found is 15
```

The last step is to increase the units value, create an XML representation of the data, and store it into a file.

You know that Scala does not require you to stuff XML elements into a string. But, you may wonder, how do you generate dynamic content into an XML document? This is where the smarts of the Scala XML library goes beyond what you've seen so far. You can embed Scala expressions within any XML fragment. So, if we write <symbol ticker={tickerSymbol}/>, then Scala will replace {tickerSymbol} with the value of the variable tickerSymbol and result in an element like <symbol ticker="AAPL"/>. You can place any Scala code in between the {},[2] and that block can result in a value, an element, or a sequence of elements. Let's put this feature to use to create an XML representation from the Map we created previously. When done, we'll save the content into a file using the save() method of the XML object. Let's look at the code for this:

UsingScala/ReadWriteXML.scala

```
val updatedStocksAndUnitsXML =
<symbols>
  { stocksAndUnitsMap.map { updateUnitsAndCreateXML } }
</symbols>

def updateUnitsAndCreateXML(element : (String, Int)) = {
  val (ticker, units) = element
  <symbol ticker={ticker}>
    <units>{units + 1}</units>
  </symbol>
}

XML save ("stocks2.xml", updatedStocksAndUnitsXML)
println("The saved file contains " +
  (XML.load("stocks2.xml") \\ "symbol").size + " symbol elements")
```

The output from the previous code is shown here:

```
The saved file contains 15 symbol elements
```

---

2. If you want to place a { in the content, escape it with an additional {. That is, {{ will result in one { in the content.

Let's examine the code that produced the previous output. We first created an XML document with symbols as the root element. The data for the child elements (symbol) we want to embed within this root element resides in stocksAndUnitsMap, which is a Map we created earlier. So, we iterate over each element of this map and create an XML representation using the yet-to-be-implemented method updateUnitsAndCreateXML(). The result of this operation is a collection of elements (since we used the map() method). Remember that in the closure attached to the map() method, Scala is implicitly sending the parameters we receive within the closure (an element of the Map) to the updateUnitsAndCreateXML() method.

Now, let's look at the updateUnitsAndCreateXML() method. It accepts an element of the Map as a parameter and creates an XML fragment of the format <symbol ticker="sym"><units>value</units></symbol>. While processing each symbol, we took care of the objective to increase units by 1.

The last step is to save the generated document, and we use the save() method to achieve that task. We read back the saved document from the file stocks2.xml to take a look at the content we generated.

The save() method simply saved the XML document without any bells and whistles. If you'd like to add an XML version, add doctypes, and specify encoding, use one of the variations of the save() method on the XML singleton object.

14.6 Getting Stock Prices from the Web

The final step to complete our net asset application is to get the stock price from the Web. We have the list of ticker symbols and the units in the file stocks.xml we saw earlier. For each of these symbols, we need to fetch the closing price. Thankfully, Yahoo provides a web service that we can use to get stock data. To find the latest closing price for Google stocks, for example, we can visit the following URL:

```
http://ichart.finance.yahoo.com/table.csv?s=GOOG&a=00&b=01&c=2009
```

The parameters s, a, b, and c represent the ticker symbol, start month (January is 0), start day, and start year, respectively. If you don't specify the end dates using the parameters d, e, and f, the service returns all prices from the given start date until the most recent available date. When you visit the previous URL, you'll get a comma-separated value (CSV) file to download.

A sample of the file is shown here:

```
Date,Open,High,Low,Close,Volume,Adj Close
2009-04-02,363.31,369.76,360.32,362.50,4488000,362.50
2009-04-01,343.78,355.24,340.61,354.09,3301200,354.09
2009-03-31,348.93,353.51,346.18,348.06,3655300,348.06
...
```

To get the latest closing price, we have to skip the first header line and step to the second line, containing the data for the most recent date. From among the comma-separated values, simply grab the fifth element[3] (the element at index 4 starting the count with the traditional 0).

Let's put the Yahoo service to work. We'll open our stocks.xml file,[4] grab each symbol, and fetch the latest closing price for that ticker. We multiply the closing price we fetched by the number of units we have, and we get the total value for that stock. Total all those values, and we get to know the total worth of our investments.

Let's capture the code that populates a map with the ticker symbols and units present in the XML file and the code to fetch data from the Yahoo service into a singleton object named StockPriceFinder:

UsingScala/StockPriceFinder.scala

```scala
object StockPriceFinder {
  def getLatestClosingPrice(symbol: String) = {
    val url = "http://ichart.finance.yahoo.com/table.csv?s=" +
        symbol + "&a=00&b=01&c=" + new java.util.Date().getYear

    val data = scala.io.Source.fromURL(url).mkString
    val mostRecentData = data.split("\n")(1)
    val closingPrice = mostRecentData.split(",")(4).toDouble
    closingPrice
  }

  def getTickersAndUnits() = {
    val stocksAndUnitsXML = scala.xml.XML.load("stocks.xml")

    (Map[String, Int]() /: (stocksAndUnitsXML \ "symbol")) { (map, symbolNode) =>
        val ticker = (symbolNode \ "@ticker").toString
        val units = (symbolNode \ "units").text.toInt
        map(ticker) = units //Creates and returns a new Map
      }
  }
}
```

---

3. Grab the 5th element if you want the closing price or grab the 7th element if you want the adjusted closing price.

4. I'm not presenting a full example that reads from the console and updates units in the file stocks.xml. As a experienced programmer, you know already how to do that using the examples given so far in this chapter.

In the getLatestClosingPrice() method, given a symbol, we go out to the Yahoo service and get the price data. Since the data is in CSV format, we split the data to extract the closing price. The closing price is finally returned from this method.

Since our ticker symbols and units are in stocks.xml, the getTickersAndUnits() method reads this file and creates a map of ticker symbols and units. We saw in earlier sections how to accomplish this. It is the same code moved into the previous singleton object.

Now we're all set to fetch the data and compute the results. The code for that is shown here:

```
UsingScala/FindTotalWorthSequential.scala
```

```
val symbolsAndUnits = StockPriceFinder.getTickersAndUnits

println("Today is " + new java.util.Date())
println("Ticker  Units  Closing Price($) Total Value($)")

val startTime = System.nanoTime()

val netWorth = (0.0 /: symbolsAndUnits) { (worth, symbolAndUnits) =>
  val (symbol, units) = symbolAndUnits

  val latestClosingPrice = StockPriceFinder getLatestClosingPrice symbol

  val value = units * latestClosingPrice

  println("%-7s  %-5d  %-16f  %f".format(symbol, units, latestClosingPrice, value))

  worth + value
}
val endTime = System.nanoTime()

println("The total value of your investments is $" + netWorth)
println("Took %f seconds".format((endTime-startTime)/1000000000.0))
```

The output from the previous code is shown here:

```
Today is Fri Apr 03 11:14:21 MDT 2009
Ticker  Units  Closing Price($) Total Value($)
XRX     240    4.980000          1195.200000
NSM     200    11.250000         2250.000000
SYMC    230    16.020000         3684.600000
ADBE    125    23.280000         2910.000000
VRSN    200    20.070000         4014.000000
CSCO    250    18.140000         4535.000000
TXN     190    16.470000         3129.300000
ALU     150    2.010000          301.500000
IBM     215    100.820000        21676.300000
```

```
INTC      160     15.700000        2512.000000
ORCL      200     18.820000        3764.000000
HPQ       225     33.690000        7580.250000
AMD       150     3.160000         474.000000
AAPL      200     112.710000       22542.000000
MSFT      190     19.290000        3665.100000
The total value of your investments is $84233.25
Took 18.146055 seconds
```

In the previous code, we first get the map of ticker symbols and units from the StockPriceFinder. Then, for each symbol, we request that the StockPriceFinder get the latest price using the getLatestClosingPrice() method. Once we receive the latest closing price, we multiply it with the units to find the total value for that stock. We use the /:()—foldLeft()—method to help iterate and find the net worth at the same time.

We didn't need much code to accomplish the task. The previous example took about eighteen seconds to run. In the next section, we'll make it respond faster.

14.7 Making the Net Asset Application Concurrent

The sequential implementation of the net asset application looked up the latest price for each symbol one at a time. The major delay is the time spent waiting for the responses from the Web—the network delay. Let's refactor the previous code so we can make the requests for the latest prices for all the symbols concurrently. When done, we should see a faster response from our net asset application.

To make this application concurrent, we will place the calls to getLatest-ClosingPrice() in separate actors. Once they receive the response, they can send a message to the main actor. The main actor can then receive all the responses and total the net worth. This part will be sequential. Here is the code to achieve this goal:

```
UsingScala/FindTotalWorthConcurrent.scala
import scala.actors._
import Actor._

val symbolsAndUnits = StockPriceFinder.getTickersAndUnits

val caller = self

println("Today is " + new java.util.Date())
println("Ticker  Units  Closing Price($) Total Value($)")

val startTime = System.nanoTime()
```

```scala
symbolsAndUnits.keys.foreach { symbol =>
  actor { caller ! (symbol, StockPriceFinder.getLatestClosingPrice(symbol)) }
}

val netWorth = (0.0 /: (1 to symbolsAndUnits.size)) { (worth, index) =>
  receiveWithin(10000) {
    case (symbol : String, latestClosingPrice: Double) =>
    val units = symbolsAndUnits(symbol)
    val value = units * latestClosingPrice
    println("%-7s  %-5d  %-16f  %f".format(
      symbol, units, latestClosingPrice, value))
    worth + value
  }
}

val endTime = System.nanoTime()

println("The total value of your investments is $" + netWorth)
println("Took %f seconds".format((endTime-startTime)/1000000000.0))
```

The output from the previous code is shown here:

```
Today is Fri Apr 03 11:18:35 MDT 2009
Ticker  Units  Closing Price($) Total Value($)
ADBE     125    23.280000           2910.000000
XRX      240    4.980000            1195.200000
SYMC     230    16.020000           3684.600000
VRSN     200    20.070000           4014.000000
CSCO     250    18.140000           4535.000000
ALU      150    2.010000            301.500000
NSM      200    11.250000           2250.000000
TXN      190    16.470000           3129.300000
IBM      215    100.820000          21676.300000
INTC     160    15.700000           2512.000000
ORCL     200    18.820000           3764.000000
HPQ      225    33.690000           7580.250000
AAPL     200    112.710000          22542.000000
MSFT     190    19.290000           3665.100000
AMD      150    3.160000            474.000000
The total value of your investments is $84233.25
Took 7.683939 seconds
```

Review the previous code to make sure you understand what's going on. We have put to use the concepts you have learned so far in this book in order to get the previous code working.

As you can see from the previous output, the net asset value is the same[5] as in the sequential execution. However, the concurrent version took only about seven seconds vs. the eighteen seconds the sequential

---

5. Sorry, Scala code does not increase our net asset, but I contend it increases our professional worth!

version took. Go ahead and try these two versions on your machine, and observe the results. Each day you run it, the result will be different because of fluctuating stock prices and network traffic.

14.8 Putting a GUI on the Net Asset Application

You're eager to show off your net asset application to friends, but you know that a GUI will make it more appealing. The good news is that Scala comes with the scala.swing library that makes it easy to write Swing applications in Scala. Let's understand some basics and then quickly put a GUI on our application.

The scala.swing library has a singleton object named SimpleGUIApplication. This object already has a main() method. It expects you to implement a top() method in which you'd return an instance of the all-too-familiar Frame. So, implementing a Swing application is as simple as extending SimpleGUIApplication and implementing the top() method. How do you handle events? You handle them with style—rather than the mundane listener methods, you will use the idiomatic pattern matching to handle events. An example will help put all this in perspective. So, here is the code:

UsingScala/SampleGUI.scala

```scala
import scala.swing._
import event._

object SampleGUI extends SimpleGUIApplication {
  def top = new MainFrame {
    title = "A Sample Scala Swing GUI"

    val label = new Label { text = "------------"}
    val button = new Button { text = "Click me" }

    contents = new FlowPanel {
      contents += label
      contents += button
    }

    listenTo(button)

    reactions += {
      case ButtonClicked(button) =>
        label.text = "You clicked!"
    }
  }
}
```

Go ahead, compile the previous code using scalac SampleGUI.scala, and then run it using the command scala SampleGUI. The initial window that pops up is shown here on the left. The effect of clicking the button is shown on the right.

We extended our singleton object SampleGUI from SimpleGUIApplication and provided the implementation for the top() method. Within this method we create an instance of an anonymous class that extends Main-Frame. The MainFrame class is part of the Scala swing library and takes care of shutting down the framework and quitting the application in addition to serving as a main application window. So, unlike the Swing JFrame, when using MainFrame, you don't have to deal with the default-CloseOperation property to close the windows.

We then set a title property and created an instance of a Label and a Button. The contents property of MainFrame represents the content that the main window will hold. It can contain only one component and in this example holds the instance of FlowPanel. We then add (using the append method +=()) the label and button we created to the contents property of the FlowPanel instance. As you can imagine, the FlowPanel, like its AWT/Swing counterpart java.awt.Flowlayout, arranges its components horizontally, one after the other.

The last order of business is to handle the events, in this example, the events on the button. We register the button as a source of an event by calling the listenTo() method; that is, we're asking the main window to listen to the button events. We then register the event handler by providing a partial function to the reactions property. Within the handler, we match the events we're interested in using the appropriate case classes for events. In this example, that would be the click event on the button, and we use the ButtonClicked case class to match it.

Now let's focus our attention on putting a GUI on top of the net asset application. There is one complication you should pay attention to. When we create multiple actors to query for the prices, remember to update the GUI components only from the main UI owning thread. That's because the UI components in Swing are not thread safe. So, let's get down to writing the code.

When we finish this example, the GUI will look like the following:

Ticker	Units	Price	Value
XRX	240	?	?
NSM	200	?	?
SYMC	230	?	?
ADBE	125	?	?
VRSN	200	?	?
CSCO	250	?	?
TXN	190	?	?
ALU	150	?	?
IBM	215	?	?
INTC	160	?	?
ORCL	200	?	?
HPQ	225	?	?
AMD	150	?	?
AAPL	200	?	?
MSFT	190	?	?

Net Asset — Last updated: ----- — Update — Net Asset: ????

The table displays the ticker symbols, units, price, and total value for each stock a user holds. At the bottom, you will eventually see the net asset value, and at the top you'll see the last time the price was updated. The Update button will start the action to get the data from the Web.

Part of the code we will write will deal with the GUI components. The rest of the code will deal with sending requests to the Yahoo service and receiving the responses using the StockPriceFinder we wrote earlier. Once we get those responses, we will have to compute the value of each stock and the net assets—that's our business logic. I'm sure you'd like to keep the code cohesive by separating the business logic from the code that manipulates the GUI components. So, let's first take a look at the singleton object NetAssetStockPriceHelper that will handle the business logic and act as a liaison between the GUI and StockPriceFinder:

UsingScala/NetAssetStockPriceHelper.scala

```
import scala.actors._
import Actor._

object NetAssetStockPriceHelper {
  val symbolsAndUnits = StockPriceFinder.getTickersAndUnits

  def getInitialTableValues : Array[Array[Any]] = {
    val emptyArrayOfArrayOfAny = new Array[Array[Any]](0,0)
```

```
    (emptyArrayOfArrayOfAny /: symbolsAndUnits) { (data, element) =>
      val (symbol, units) = element
      data ++ Array(List(symbol, units, "?", "?").toArray)
    }
  }

  def fetchPrice(updater: Actor) = actor {

  val caller = self

  symbolsAndUnits.keys.foreach { symbol =>
    actor { caller ! (symbol, StockPriceFinder.getLatestClosingPrice(symbol)) }
  }

  val netWorth = (0.0 /: (1 to symbolsAndUnits.size)) { (worth, index) =>
    receiveWithin(10000) {
      case (symbol : String, latestClosingPrice: Double) =>
      val units = symbolsAndUnits(symbol)
      val value = units * latestClosingPrice
      updater ! (symbol, units, latestClosingPrice, value)
      worth + value
    }
  }

    updater ! netWorth
  }
}
```

The getInitialTableValues() method returns a two-dimensional array to fill in the table with initial values. It includes the ticker symbol and the units. Since the price and value is not known initially, this method returns ? for those places.

The fetchPrice() method accepts a UI updating actor as a parameter, and the return value from this method is an actor as well. The parameter actor will be responsible on the UI side for updating the UI components in the UI thread. The actor this method returns does two things. First, it sends concurrent request to the StockPriceFinder to go out and get the price for various symbols. Second, as it receives the response, it computes the stock value and immediately sends it to the UI updating actor so it can update the UI right away. Furthermore, it continues to receive the remaining prices and determines the net asset. When all the prices are received, it sends the net asset to the UI updating actor so it can display that amount. As you read through this method, you'll notice it is like the code you saw earlier in Section 14.7, *Making the Net Asset Application Concurrent*, on page 195. The main difference is while the latter printed out the result, fetchPrice() sends the details to the UI updating actor so it can display on the GUI.

Now the only task left is to write the GUI code to talk to NetAssetStock-PriceHelper. Let's first start with the class definition:

UsingScala/NetAssetAppGUI.scala

```
import scala.swing._
import event._
import scala.actors._
import Actor._
import java.awt.Color

object NetAssetAppGUI extends SimpleGUIApplication {
  def top = mainFrame
```

We've created a singleton object named NetAssetAPPGUI that extends the SimpleGUIApplication. We've defined the required top() method. It returns a value mainFrame that we'll define soon. Let's now take a look at creating an instance of MainFrame:

UsingScala/NetAssetAppGUI.scala

```
val mainFrame = new MainFrame {
  title = "Net Asset"

  val dateLabel = new Label { text = "Last updated: ----- " }

  val valuesTable = new Table(
      NetAssetStockPriceHelper.getInitialTableValues,
      Array("Ticker", "Units", "Price", "Value")) {
    showGrid = true
    gridColor = Color.BLACK
  }

  val updateButton = new Button { text = "Update" }
  val netAssetLabel = new Label { text = "Net Asset: ????" }
```

We set the desired title value and created the four components we need: two labels, one table, and one button. Creating the labels and buttons is quite straightforward. Let's focus on the table here. We created an instance of scala.swing.Table and sent two arguments to its constructor. The first argument is the initial data for the table that we obtain from the NetAssetStockPriceHelper's getInitialTableValues() method. The second argument consists of the names for the column headers.

Remember, we can't place multiple components on the main window.

So, we will place these components within a BoxPanel and in turn place the BoxPanel into the contents of the main frame, as shown here:

UsingScala/NetAssetAppGUI.scala

```
contents = new BoxPanel(Orientation.Vertical) {
  contents += dateLabel
  contents += valuesTable
  contents += new ScrollPane(valuesTable)

  contents += new FlowPanel {
    contents += updateButton
    contents += netAssetLabel
  }
}
```

The BoxPanel boxes up or stacks up the components given to it (especially since the orientation is vertical). We put the dateLabel on the top, followed by the table. At the bottom we place a FlowPanel that holds the other label and the button.

We're almost done. The only thing left is to handle the events and update the UI:

UsingScala/NetAssetAppGUI.scala

```
listenTo(updateButton)

reactions += {
  case ButtonClicked(button) =>
    button.enabled = false
    NetAssetStockPriceHelper fetchPrice uiUpdater
}
```

In the previous code we subscribed to events on the button and added a handler. In the handler we first disable the Update button and then send a request to the NetAssetStockPriceHelper to go get the prices and compute the value. We provide to it a uiUpdater, which is an actor we will create soon. Remember that since the method fetchPrice() returns an actor, the request is processed in a separate thread, and the previous call is nonblocking. At this point, the NetAssetStockPriceHelper will concurrently request stock prices and compute the value. As soon as the first price arrives, it will start sending messages to the uiUpdater. So, we better create that one quickly so we can start updating the UI.

```scala
val uiUpdater = new Actor {
  def act = {
    loop {
      react {
        case (symbol : String, units : Int, price : Double, value : Double) =>
          updateTable(symbol, units, price, value)
        case netAsset =>
          netAssetLabel.text = "Net Asset: " + netAsset
          dateLabel.text = "Last updated: " + new java.util.Date()
          updateButton.enabled = true
      }
    }
  }

  override protected def scheduler() = new SingleThreadedScheduler
}

uiUpdater.start()
```

The value uiUpdater refers to an anonymous instance of an Actor. Once we call start() on it, it will run in the main event dispatch thread since we have overridden the scheduler() method to return an instance of SingleThreadedScheduler. In the act() method, we receive the messages sent by the NetAssetStockPriceHelper and update the UI components appropriately. That last missing piece is the updateTable() method, which will update the table with data as it arrives. Here's that method along with the braces at the end to complete the code we've been developing:

```scala
  def updateTable(symbol: String, units : Int, price : Double, value : Double) {
    for(i <- 0 until valuesTable.rowCount) {
      if (valuesTable(i, 0) == symbol) {
        valuesTable(i, 2) = price
        valuesTable(i, 3) = value
      }
    }
  }
}
```

The previous method simply loops through the table, locates the symbol of interest, and updates the row. We can devise other means to look up the table if we desire to improve this. For instance, we may store the row number in a map as we initially populate a table. Then we can quickly locate the row by performing a lookup on that map.

Now as you run the application, you will notice the stock prices and values are updated as they arrive, as shown in the following figure:

Net Asset			
Last updated: -----			
Ticker	Units	Price	Value
XRX	240	?	?
NSM	200	14.47	2,894
SYMC	230	15.88	3,652.4
ADBE	125	?	?
VRSN	200	?	?
CSCO	250	?	?
TXN	190	?	?
ALU	150	?	?
IBM	215	?	?
INTC	160	?	?
ORCL	200	?	?
HPQ	225	?	?
AMD	150	?	?
AAPL	200	?	?
MSFT	190	?	?

Update   Net Asset: ????

Once all the prices are received, the net asset and the time are updated, as shown here:

Net Asset			
Last updated: Thu Jun 11 20:38:06 MDT 2009			
Ticker	Units	Price	Value
XRX	240	7	1,680
NSM	200	14.47	2,894
SYMC	230	15.88	3,652.4
ADBE	125	30.4	3,800
VRSN	200	19.24	3,848
CSCO	250	20.1	5,025
TXN	190	20.84	3,959.6
ALU	150	2.87	430.5
IBM	215	109.4	23,521
INTC	160	16.35	2,616
ORCL	200	20.94	4,188
HPQ	225	37.23	8,376.75
AMD	150	4.7	705
AAPL	200	139.95	27,990
MSFT	190	22.83	4,337.7

Update   Net Asset: 97023.95

The code we've created so far follows a happy path. If you have a network connection and if the service responded on time, everything goes well. In reality that is not always the case. You will have to handle exceptions within the actors and propagate the failure back to the uiUpdater actor so it can display the message on the UI. For this, you could add another case statement that accepts an exception message, and of course the actors will have to send those messages when they hit the failure situations.

For your benefit, I've listed the entire code for the UI here again—you may be surprised how succinct the code is:

`UsingScala/NetAssetAppGUI.scala`

```scala
import scala.swing._
import event._
import scala.actors._
import Actor._
import java.awt.Color

object NetAssetAppGUI extends SimpleGUIApplication {
  def top = mainFrame

  val mainFrame = new MainFrame {
    title = "Net Asset"

    val dateLabel = new Label { text = "Last updated: ----- " }

    val valuesTable = new Table(
      NetAssetStockPriceHelper.getInitialTableValues,
      Array("Ticker", "Units", "Price", "Value")) {
      showGrid = true
      gridColor = Color.BLACK
    }

    val updateButton = new Button { text = "Update" }
    val netAssetLabel = new Label { text = "Net Asset: ????" }

    contents = new BoxPanel(Orientation.Vertical) {
      contents += dateLabel
      contents += valuesTable
      contents += new ScrollPane(valuesTable)

      contents += new FlowPanel {
        contents += updateButton
        contents += netAssetLabel
      }
    }

    listenTo(updateButton)

    reactions += {
      case ButtonClicked(button) =>
        button.enabled = false
        NetAssetStockPriceHelper fetchPrice uiUpdater
    }
```

```scala
val uiUpdater = new Actor {
  def act = {
    loop {
      react {
        case (symbol : String, units : Int, price : Double, value : Double) =>
          updateTable(symbol, units, price, value)
        case netAsset =>
          netAssetLabel.text = "Net Asset: " + netAsset
          dateLabel.text = "Last updated: " + new java.util.Date()
          updateButton.enabled = true
      }
    }
  }

  override protected def scheduler() = new SingleThreadedScheduler
}

uiUpdater.start()

def updateTable(symbol: String, units : Int, price : Double, value : Double) {
  for(i <- 0 until valuesTable.rowCount) {
    if (valuesTable(i, 0) == symbol) {
      valuesTable(i, 2) = price
      valuesTable(i, 3) = value
    }
  }
}
    }
  }
}
```

In this chapter, you saw firsthand the conciseness and expressiveness of Scala. You enjoyed the benefits of pattern matching, XML processing, and functional style. You also saw the benefit and ease of the concurrency API. You're all set to take these benefits to your real-word projects. Thank you for reading.

Appendix A

Web Resources

A Brief History of Scala...
        ... http://www.artima.com/weblogs/viewpost.jsp?thread=163733
Martin Odersky talks about creating Scala.

Canary Test...
        ... http://memeagora.blogspot.com/2007/06/coalmine-canary-tests.html
In this blog, Neal Ford discusses canary tests and the advantage of starting out small and simple.

Command Query Separation...
        ... http://www.martinfowler.com/bliki/CommandQuerySeparation.html
In this blog, Martin Fowler discusses the term *command query separation.*

Continuous Integration...
        ... http://martinfowler.com/articles/continuousIntegration.html
In this article, Martin Fowler discusses the practice of continuous integration.

Discussion Forum for This Book http://forums.pragprog.com/forums/87
This is the discussion forum for this book where readers share their opinions, ask questions, respond to questions, and interact with each other.

Essence vs. Ceremony...
        ... http://blog.thinkrelevance.com/2008/4/1/ending-legacy-code-in-our-lifetime
In this blog titled "Ending Legacy Code in Our Lifetime," Stuart Halloway discusses essence vs. ceremony.

Fractal Programming...
        ... http://ola-bini.blogspot.com/2008/06/fractal-programming.html
Ola Bini makes a case for mixing different languages to build large-scale applications with multiple layers including the domain layer, the dynamic layer, and the stable layer.

Hittin' the Edge Cases.... http://blogs.sun.com/navi/entry/scala_puzzlers_part_1
Ivan Tarasov discusses some Scala puzzlers, including a problem with parameterless case classes.

Java SE.......................... http://java.sun.com/javase/downloads/index.jsp
This is the download page for Java SE versions.

Lift Webframework.. http://liftweb.net
This is David Pollak's Lift Webframework built using Scala.

Loan Pattern.......................... http://scala.sygneca.com/patterns/loan
This is the Scala wiki page describing the Loan pattern—a pattern to dispose of nonmemory resources automatically.

Polyglot Programming...
.... http://memeagora.blogspot.com/2006/12/polyglot-programming.html
Neal Ford talks about Polyglot Programming.

Prefer Conciseness over Terseness.............. http://tinyurl.com/5bawat
In this blog, I discuss conciseness vs. terseness with testing as an example.

ScalaTest.................................... http://www.artima.com/scalatest
This is a testing framework written in Scala to test Scala and Java code.

Scala IDE Plug-ins............. http://www.scala-lang.org/node/91\#ide_plugins
This page presents details of IDE plug-ins available for working with Scala.

Scala Language Specification...
.... http://www.scala-lang.org/docu/files/ScalaReference.pdf
The Scala Language Specification was written by Martin Odersky of Programming Methods Laboratory, EPFL, Switzerland.

Scala Language Website.......................... http://www.scala-lang.org
This is the official website for the Scala programming language.

The Scala Language API.... http://www.scala-lang.org/docu/files/api/index.html
This is the online version of the Scala Language API.

Appendix B

Bibliography

[Arm07]   Joe Armstrong. *Programming Erlang: Software for a Concurrent World*. The Pragmatic Programmers, LLC, Raleigh, NC, and Dallas, TX, 2007.

[Bec96]   Kent Beck. *Smalltalk Best Practice Patterns*. Prentice Hall, Englewood Cliffs, NJ, 1996.

[Blo01]   Joshua Bloch. *Effective Java Programming Language Guide*. Addison Wesley Longman, Reading, MA, 2001.

[Blo08]   Joshua Bloch. *Effective Java*. Addison Wesley Longman, Reading, MA, second edition, 2008.

[Cla04]   Mike Clark. *Pragmatic Project Automation. How to Build, Deploy, and Monitor Java Applications*. The Pragmatic Programmers, LLC, Raleigh, NC, and Dallas, TX, 2004.

[DMG07]   Paul Duvall, Steve Matyas, and Andrew Glover. *Continuous Integration: Improving Software Quality and Reducing Risk*. Addison-Wesley, Reading, MA, 2007.

[For08]   Neal Ford. *The Productive Programmer*. O'Reilly & Associates, Inc, 2008.

[Fri97]   Jeffrey E. F. Friedl. *Mastering Regular Expressions*. O'Reilly & Associates, Inc, Sebastopol, CA, 1997.

[GHJV95]   Erich Gamma, Richard Helm, Ralph Johnson, and John Vlissides. *Design Patterns: Elements of Reusable Object-Oriented Software*. Addison-Wesley, Reading, MA, 1995.

[Goe06]   Brian Goetz. *Java Concurrency in Practice*. Addison-Wesley, Reading, MA, 2006.

[HT00]   Andrew Hunt and David Thomas. *The Pragmatic Programmer: From Journeyman to Master*. Addison-Wesley, Reading, MA, 2000.

[Lea00]   Doug Lea. *Concurrent Programming in Java, Second Edition: Design Principles and Patterns*. Addison-Wesley, Reading, MA, 2000.

[OSV08]   Martin Odersky, Lex Spoon, and Bill Venners. *Programming in Scala*. 2008.

[VWWA96]   Robert Virding, Claes Wikstrom, Mike Williams, and Joe Armstrong. *Concurrent Programming in Erlang*. Prentice Hall, Englewood Cliffs, NJ, second edition, 1996.

Index

The Pragmatic Bookshelf

Available in paperback and DRM-free PDF, our titles are here to help you stay on top of your game. The following are in print as of June 2009; be sure to check our website at pragprog.com for newer titles.

Title	Year	ISBN	Pages
Advanced Rails Recipes: 84 New Ways to Build Stunning Rails Apps	2008	9780978739225	464
Agile Retrospectives: Making Good Teams Great	2006	9780977616640	200
Agile Web Development with Rails, Third Edition	2009	9781934356166	784
Augmented Reality: A Practical Guide	2008	9781934356036	328
Behind Closed Doors: Secrets of Great Management	2005	9780976694021	192
Best of Ruby Quiz	2006	9780976694076	304
Core Animation for Mac OS X and the iPhone: Creating Compelling Dynamic User Interfaces	2008	9781934356104	200
Data Crunching: Solve Everyday Problems using Java, Python, and More	2005	9780974514079	208
Deploying Rails Applications: A Step-by-Step Guide	2008	9780978739201	280
Design Accessible Web Sites: 36 Keys to Creating Content for All Audiences and Platforms	2007	9781934356029	336
Desktop GIS: Mapping the Planet with Open Source Tools	2008	9781934356067	368
Developing Facebook Platform Applications with Rails	2008	9781934356128	200
Enterprise Integration with Ruby	2006	9780976694069	360
Enterprise Recipes with Ruby and Rails	2008	9781934356234	416
Everyday Scripting with Ruby: for Teams, Testers, and You	2007	9780977616619	320
FXRuby: Create Lean and Mean GUIs with Ruby	2008	9781934356074	240
From Java To Ruby: Things Every Manager Should Know	2006	9780976694090	160
GIS for Web Developers: Adding Where to Your Web Applications	2007	9780974514093	275
Google Maps API, V2: Adding Where to Your Applications	2006	PDF-Only	83
Groovy Recipes: Greasing the Wheels of Java	2008	9780978739294	264
Hello, Android: Introducing Google's Mobile Development Platform	2008	9781934356173	200
Interface Oriented Design	2006	9780976694052	240
Land the Tech Job You Love	2009	9781934356265	280
Learn to Program, 2nd Edition	2009	9781934356364	230

Continued on next page

Title	Year	ISBN	Pages
Manage It! Your Guide to Modern Pragmatic Project Management	2007	9780978739249	360
Mastering Dojo: JavaScript and Ajax Tools for Great Web Experiences	2008	9781934356111	568
No Fluff Just Stuff 2006 Anthology	2006	9780977616664	240
No Fluff Just Stuff 2007 Anthology	2007	9780978739287	320
Practical Programming: An Introduction to Computer Science Using Python	2009	9781934356272	350
Practices of an Agile Developer	2006	9780974514086	208
Pragmatic Project Automation: How to Build, Deploy, and Monitor Java Applications	2004	9780974514031	176
Pragmatic Thinking and Learning: Refactor Your Wetware	2008	9781934356050	288
Pragmatic Unit Testing in C# with NUnit	2007	9780977616671	176
Pragmatic Unit Testing in Java with JUnit	2003	9780974514017	160
Pragmatic Version Control Using Git	2008	9781934356159	200
Pragmatic Version Control using CVS	2003	9780974514000	176
Pragmatic Version Control using Subversion	2006	9780977616657	248
Programming Clojure	2009	9781934356333	304
Programming Erlang: Software for a Concurrent World	2007	9781934356005	536
Programming Groovy: Dynamic Productivity for the Java Developer	2008	9781934356098	320
Programming Ruby: The Pragmatic Programmers' Guide, Second Edition	2004	9780974514055	864
Programming Ruby 1.9: The Pragmatic Programmers' Guide	2009	9781934356081	960
Prototype and script.aculo.us: You Never Knew JavaScript Could Do This!	2007	9781934356012	448
Rails Recipes	2006	9780977616602	350
Rails for .NET Developers	2008	9781934356203	300
Rails for Java Developers	2007	9780977616695	336
Rails for PHP Developers	2008	9781934356043	432
Rapid GUI Development with QtRuby	2005	PDF-Only	83
Release It! Design and Deploy Production-Ready Software	2007	9780978739218	368
Scripted GUI Testing with Ruby	2008	9781934356180	192
Ship it! A Practical Guide to Successful Software Projects	2005	9780974514048	224
Stripes ...and Java Web Development Is Fun Again	2008	9781934356210	375
TextMate: Power Editing for the Mac	2007	9780978739232	208
The Definitive ANTLR Reference: Building Domain-Specific Languages	2007	9780978739256	384

Continued on next page